THE DAY SOON DAWNS

A FINNISH SAILOR'S TRUE STORY OF SURVIVING STUTTHOF

—ɱ—

A Family Memoir

LIISA KOVALA

Contact Liisa Kovala at
http://www.liisakovala.com

ISBN-13: 978-1505381290
ISBN-10: 1505381290
Library of Congress Control Number: 2014921779
CreateSpace Independent Publishing Platform
North Charleston, South Carolina

For Isä and Äiti
and
Mia and Kieran

Only guard yourself and guard your soul carefully, lest you forget the things your eyes saw, and lest these things depart your heart all the days of your life, and you shall make them known to your children, and to your children's children.

—Deuteronomy 4:9

Never, never, aged father,
Never, thou, beloved mother,
Never, ye, my kindred spirits,
Never harbour care, nor sorrow,
Never fall to bitter weeping,
Since thy child has gone to others,
To the distant home of strangers

—Rune XXIV, *The Kalevala*

Contents

Prologue

—ᴍ—

OUR JOURNEY TOGETHER BEGAN on a cold Sunday afternoon in January, typical of Northern Ontario, on the first of what would be many weekly visits to my parents' house in search of my father's memories. The small, brick bungalow was cozy and warm, although the temperature outside had plummeted. The picture window framed a view of the yard blanketed by a thick layer of snow, extending out to cover the ice on St. Charles Lake like a pristine sheet of paper. The sun bounced off the stark, white landscape and caught the light in the flecks blown from the rooftop. The familiar smell of coffee and fresh cardamom from my mother's homemade *pulla*, a traditional Finnish coffee bread, wafted in from the kitchen.

Since I was a child, I'd heard fragments of my father's story, but foolishly I'd paid little attention. A natural storyteller, he was always conscious of his impressionable young listeners and avoided anything that might be too traumatic. Now, as an adult, I wanted to know what life had been like for my father in faraway Finland and Poland in the 1930s and '40s. As I prepared to write, I resolved not to let my father's stories evaporate into the air. I needed to preserve each droplet, to join them with the thousands of others in a river of memories from witnesses around the world. I wanted to be able to tell my children and grandchildren what really happened, something more than partial recollections from childhood of dinnertime conversations.

After almost seventy years, he was ready to share his stories, and I, comfortably seated with my feet tucked under me, laptop propped on my knees, was anxious to hear them. But how much would he remember? Was he ready to return to those dark times? Was I prepared to hear about the horrors?

Across from me, my eighty-three-year-old father, Aarne Kovala, sat in his faded, blue armchair. Before me he placed a plain, white shoebox that I had coveted as a young girl. I picked it up and noticed it smelled faintly of dust and mildew, but when I removed the lid, the images inside were as fresh and crisp as the day they were taken. I was astounded to find a collection of black and white photographs, postcards of ships, several passports, and seamen's union cards, amongst other treasures. He had stuffed several decades of his life into this little container. Each piece represented a story or would trigger a recollection. I knew if I asked the right questions, one by one the memories in the shoebox would come to life.

My father had not yet spoken. He sat in his chair, large forearms resting on his knees, back hunched forward in a posture so familiar to me. Between his thumb and forefinger, he aimlessly twisted and turned a piece of paper, as I had seen him do so many times before when he was lost in thought. His blue eyes, soft and kind, focused on something in the middle distance, the place between then and now, before he turned to look at me directly. The lines on his forehead furrowed as he shifted in his chair. Then, without warning, his eyes shone, and a smile animated his face.

He began to speak in the sing-song of his native Finnish, its long words and vowels rolling gently like waves. I looked at my mother, Anja, seated in her matching recliner. She shrugged slightly and shook her head. Were the memories of his Finnish past wrapped only in his native tongue? In that instant I regretted never having learned my parents' language.

When he finally paused, I said, "OK, Dad. But you're going to have to tell me in English."

He started again.

His story began to flow, words tripping gently in his broken English, travelling to the river of his childhood, where he and his friends spent hours riding the rapids. From there, I knew, his words would bring us to the sea, to the ship that would carry him to the port that launched his nightmares. The ripples and waves of his story would, in time, uncover what lay beneath his calm exterior. It would also deliver him home. But not yet.

Instead his story brought us to the beginning, to a small town in northern Finland and a young boy whose life was about to change forever.

CHAPTER 1
Oulu, January 1939

—⚍—

THE INNOCENCE OF YOUTH ended when bombs blasted Aarne Kovala's hometown. The raging rapids of the Oulujoki River were silent under slabs of shifting ice, the lush gardens of Ainola Park were buried under quilts of white, and the warm sands of the Baltic lay barren while fire rained from the sky. It was the first day of the new decade.

Aarne, arms laden with firewood, followed his friend, Matti Salmi, up a set of narrow stairs, delivering fuel for the Salmis' stove.

"Wait for me," he said, chin propped on top of his load as he negotiated the steps.

"We're almost there. Just another flight," Matti said through huffs of breath.

Despite the icy temperatures outside, both boys were warm from exertion, their faces flushed and legs heavy.

They were almost at the top of the steps when they heard a distinctive brat-a-tat-tat, brat-a-tat-tat from somewhere in the distance. The boys froze and looked at each other with wide eyes. Machine gun fire. They dropped the kindling on the stairs and rushed to the little window overlooking the street.

The reverberations of low-flying plane engines echoed in the wooden stairwell, filling the small space with their oppressive sounds and causing the boys to catch their breath. Above, a Russian airplane, guns and gunners visible, cast a shadow on the street below, obstructing the view of the clear afternoon sky from the small window. The boys pressed their noses against the cold glass, clawing the window ledge as they surveyed the terrifying scene.

Aarne had overheard the adults discussing their worries about a war with Russia in the months preceding the fall of the first bombs. The Russians wanted to reclaim territory lost in the Russian Civil War. On December 6, 1917, Finland had declared its independence from Russia. Now Stalin demanded that land on the border and islands in the Gulf be ceded to Russia, arguing it was to protect Leningrad, only forty kilometres away. Russia already had signed treaties of mutual assistance from Lithuania, Latvia, and Estonia and seemed to want more control over the Baltic. Finland, however, rejected Stalin's proposals. War was inevitable.

In Oulu, a small town of twenty-one thousand off the coast of the Baltic on the Gulf of Bothnia, preparations for war had been taking place for several months. Aarne's father, Jussi Kovala, was the head mechanic of Sähkölaitos, the city's hydroelectric plant. He and other concerned citizens had been gathering at the Åström Brothers leather factory to discuss what should be done if the conflict reached Oulu. Aarne learned they had decided on several measures: watch-towers to identify the locations of fallen explosives, large sandboxes to help with the outbreaks of fire, and trenches and bomb shelters for protection. Some citizens even built their own shelters out of con-crete, but most working-class families didn't have the financial re-sources and so relied on existing root cellars. There was little time or money to build enough of them by the time the war rolled its way towards the Baltic town.

On November 30, 1939, the newspapers declared war. The whole city became familiar with the chilling sounds of air raid signals, rising from a low blare to a high shriek, warning everyone to seek shelter. Every time they started, Aarne felt a mixture of excitement and dread. For many months he feared that Russian aircraft would follow the warnings.

Until now Aarne had been going to the local school with his friend, Matti. As the war continued to threaten the city, the school rarely opened. By eleven Aarne's formal schooling had ended, but his real edu-cation was just beginning.

"We'll go to my house," Aarne said to Matti over the drone of the bombers. "We can get into our root cellar if we're fast."

The boys sprinted down the stairs and pushed through the door into the bitter air. For a moment they were motionless. Chaos erupted in the streets as women grabbed the hands of their youngsters. Ducking their heads, men, women, and children scattered in all directions, frantically searching for loved ones and looking for safe havens. The air raid signal screamed. The plane engines rumbled. The ground seemed to shake.

"This way," Aarne shouted behind him.

The boys started running towards Aarne's house on the grounds of Sähkölaitos, slipping on the snow-covered cobblestones. The drones of the Russian planes propelled them forward. Every few blocks the boys glanced up to see if the planes were getting closer, ready to dodge between the buildings or jump into a nearby trench at any moment.

The two dashed past rows of shops and houses. Above they heard the sound of a plane dying, a high whine as it arced and dove in what seemed to be their direction. Aarne and Matti stopped in their tracks, squinting into the sky at the doomed aircraft.

"It's going to crash." Matti's voice was barely audible.

The boys moved back against the wall of a building, their eyes peeled on the plane.

"Look, someone's there." Aarne pointed at the silhouette of a man jumping from the bowels of the aircraft.

The dark figure, small at first against the sky, grew larger and larger as it plummeted towards the ground. After what seemed to be forever, the parachute opened, swaying the Russian back and forth until he dropped down beyond the buildings.

"There's another one," Aarne said.

Aarne and Matti scanned the sky. Several seconds passed.

"Why isn't his parachute opening?" Matti asked.

Aarne watched the figure grow larger in the sky as it sailed towards them. He was sure the parachute was going to open and deliver this Russian to safety too.

It didn't.

The soldier's body free fell through the air towards the two boys, who stood still on the sidewalk. With a tremendous thud, the Russian pilot smashed onto the street. Both boys turned away; Aarne covered his face with his hands against the horrific sight of the lifeless body, his arms and legs flayed out in unnatural positions.

For a brief moment time was suspended. No one moved. Even the air seemed still.

The silence was shattered as several men ran from nearby buildings to the body of the Russian. The men shouted at one another in a commotion of activity. From the sidewalk Aarne and Matti watched a few adults as they cut the buttons from the soldier's uniform: gruesome souvenirs.

The boys turned away from the distressing sight and raced in the direction of Sähkölaitos and the Kovala bomb shelter.

The smell of home cooking greeted them at the door of Aarne's house, and a dinner of partially eaten potatoes and roast tempted them to sit at the abandoned kitchen table.

"*Äiti* must have put out the food just as the signal started," Aarne said. He was still trembling, but he encouraged Matti with a smile. "Shouldn't let this all go to waste."

"No, that would be wrong. I'm sure your mother won't mind," Matti replied.

The boys devoured the unfinished meals.

"This is the best thing I've ever tasted," Matti said, his fork shaking in his hand.

Aarne nodded, but his mouth was too full to respond. Aarne's mother, Anna Liisa, was constantly trying to get enough food for the family, lining up at the stores with her food stamps or taking her bicycle to the outskirts of town to trade with the farmers. For a moment a sense of normalcy returned. When they had filled their stomachs, they joined the others in the bomb shelter they shared with the Raivio and Markkusela families.

When the boys opened the root cellar door, Anna Liisa smiled with relief. Aarne and Matti nodded at the other families and sat down on the dirt floor, near Aarne's siblings, before explaining what they had seen.

Aarne glanced at his brother, thirteen-year-old Kalle. He was quiet and looked paler than usual. His older brother, Veikko, was nowhere to be seen. The eldest Kovala son, Heimo, was a soldier fighting the Russians somewhere on the eastern border. Aarne's father was still at work, hopefully finding safety in one of the buildings of the hydroelectric plant.

"You must pay attention to where the bombs are landing," Lylli, ten years his senior, lectured. "Aarne, it will be your job to remind people to open up their mouths. Otherwise their eardrums might explode from the pressure."

Aarne nodded, looking up at the husky figure of his sister. She was many centimetres taller than his diminutive mother.

"I'll remember," he said confidently. He hugged his knees into his chest, looking at the families huddled together inside the damp cellar, surrounded by the smell of earth and rotting potatoes, waiting for the inevitable sound of an explosion.

As the firebombs fell, Aarne listened intently, noting their distance and the direction they were landing, like tracking thunder and lightning but less predictable.

"Getting closer now." Anna Liisa sounded calm as she regarded the boys, but she gripped her chequered apron between white-knuckled fingers. A few wisps of her brown hair strayed from her low bun.

"Keep your mouths open." Aarne shouted over the noise. His pulse quickened as he waited in anticipation.

Nearby an explosive struck. The cellar door pounded against the latches, threatening to burst open. A rush of dust flew up from the floor into the stale, dark space.

Matti coughed, and Aarne covered his nose and mouth. The dust slowly settled as the families waited.

The sounds of planes grew fainter. Aarne listened until their whir and the explosions ceased. After some time, Aarne became restless.

"Can we go out now?" He was anxious to escape the enclosed space and see the effects of the assault on the town.

Anna Liisa nodded her head. "Yes, I think it's safe. Just be careful."

Aarne pushed open the cellar door. The light reflecting off the snow temporarily blinded him as he surveyed the area for damage. The boys started walking in the direction of Aarne's house. Aarne let out a sigh of relief. His home was still standing.

—◊—

That evening the family gathered in the small kitchen. Matti had already returned home to see his mother and check for damage at his house. Anna Liisa served Jussi a cup of steaming coffee. The boys talked excitedly about what they had heard and seen until Veikko flew through the front door. He pulled off his wool coat and hat and dropped his boots by the entrance before joining the others at the table.

"Where have you been, Veikko? I was so worried about you," Anna Liisa said as she began preparing him a plate of leftovers.

"Where were you when the attack started?" Aarne asked.

"Well, Markko and I were heading home through the park," Veikko explained. Aarne and Kalle leaned in. "All of a sudden, the sirens blared. Of course we ran. But where could we go? We couldn't find a trench, and we were too far from the bomb shelters. We heard the hum of planes getting closer. We searched for cover and eventually hid under the concrete bridge. Within minutes something came whirling through the air towards us. I ducked down and covered my head with my arms. Not that it would have done any good. It was so loud. We heard an explosion only metres away. Debris was flying everywhere. A huge rock came hurtling through the air and crashed right beside us. It almost did us in. It's still there, right beside the bridge. I can show you."

"You're lucky to be alive, Veikko," Aarne said, looking at his brother with admiration and perhaps a bit of envy as well. He was grateful his family was safe.

—◊—

Several weeks passed. The citizens felt shaken, but the children tried to find fun wherever they could. A few days after the attack, Aarne and Matti found a bomb partially buried in the deep snow. They observed it for quite some time, trying to decide what to do.

"Let's pick it up," Aarne said.

Matti looked at Aarne like he was crazy. "What if it explodes?"

"Nah, I doubt it. Besides, I'll be careful."

Aarne stooped down and gently brushed the snow from around its surface. He moved slowly, just in case.

"Let's bring it to my house. My father will know what to do with it."

The boys trudged through the thick snow, towards Sähkölaitos. When they arrived at the house Matti knocked on the door. Anna Liisa opened it, drying her hands on her apron.

"Hurry inside, boys. It's cold out there," she said as a rush of icy air swirled through the entrance.

"Look what we found," Aarne said with a wide grin. With his free hand, he opened his jacket, exposing the bomb cradled in his arm.

"Where did you get that?" Kalle asked. He moved closer to get a good look, his thick eyebrows arching.

"You have a bomb? Why are you bringing it into my house?" Anna Liisa's eyes opened wide. "Jussi, you better come here."

Jussi strolled into the room, a newspaper rolled under his arm, wondering about the commotion.

He glanced down at the device and then up at the boys. The colour drained from his face.

"What do we have here, boys?" he asked. His voice was slow and steady.

One look at his expression and Aarne thought his father might pass out on the floor. He carefully placed the explosive on the kitchen table. For a moment they all stared at it in silence. No one dared to move.

"What are we going to do with it, *Isä*?" Kalle asked his father. "Maybe we should blow it up."

"Quiet, now." Jussi exhaled gradually as he began to disassemble the bomb.

The spectators held their breath. The boys watched in fascination, leaning over the kitchen table as though observing a doctor conduct surgery.

"You boys need to be more careful. These are not toys, you know," Jussi reprimanded.

As Jussi glanced at his shocked wife, Aarne noticed a smile play around his lips.

"Don't worry. It wouldn't have exploded," Aarne heard him whisper to Anna Liisa. "The firebomb was disabled when it hit the ground."

He watched his mother shake her head before leaving the kitchen. His father returned his attention to inspecting every part of the bomb with the curious boys.

—⋙—

Over the following weeks, Aarne, Matti, and Kalle, along with a few other friends, searched for more unexploded devices. One day they took several and went to Aarne's old Kuusiluoto neighbourhood, where they started a bonfire and then gathered more wood and anything else they could find to keep it blazing.

"Use a stick to roll the bomb into the fire," Kalle said.

Aarne dusted snow from a long branch and nudged it into the flames. At first nothing happened. He waited.

"I think it needs to be hotter," Matti suggested.

The boys gathered more firewood. Aarne stoked the blaze with his stick. The fire intensified. The heat made him step back, but nothing else happened. He watched the flames flicker and crackle.

"Why isn't it working?" Kalle wondered.

The boys stared at the blazing fire, the device in its centre.

"Maybe we should try something else," Aarne said.

One of the boys produced a steel plate. Using a few long sticks, they fished the bomb from the fire and rolled it on the disc before pushing the contraption back into the flames. They waited. And waited some more.

Sparks began to fly.

"Wow, just look at that." Matti moved back from the blaze.

The boys were delighted but followed Matti's lead and moved farther away, just in case.

"It's amazing." Aarne was unable to look away from the display.

The fire danced and flickered, turning a spectacular array of colours, like the northern lights that sometimes rippled in the winter sky. It was strange and captivating, its beauty and power like nothing he had ever witnessed. Aarne glanced at the faces of his friends as they stood together in the deep snow in the dead of winter, watching the fire from the Soviet bombs blaze before their eyes.

CHAPTER 2
Oulu, 1939–1942

⎯⎯⏳⎯⎯

ONLY THREE WEEKS HAD passed since Oulu was first attacked. The last air raid had killed four citizens and destroyed sixteen buildings. This time the Red Army's incendiaries were spreading chaos throughout the city. Aarne knew his father feared that if they couldn't get the fires under control, the blaze would spread.

"What do you think you're doing?" Aarne looked up to see one of the administrators of the Åström Brothers leather factory shouting at his father. "Don't worry about that warehouse. You need to stop the fire in the offices," the administrator said, pointing at a nearby building. "All of the documents are in there."

"We'll do our best," his father reassured the man, who began pacing back and forth, leaving sooty footsteps in the snow. "Doesn't look good, though."

The administrator looked frantic as he watched the flames licking the sky. Jussi and the other men would have to work feverishly to save the factory buildings.

Jussi dragged the hose over his shoulder, and Aarne and others ran over to help. Jussi struggled to get the heavy pump placed in the river, below the thick ice. It was a cold and dangerous job.

The administration office was a three-storey building; its roof was already ablaze. The flames mesmerized Aarne. Before the hose was in place, disaster struck. He watched as the roof collapsed, crashing down in a blaze of red and orange. A wall of snow flew up, slamming the spectators with such force that it threw him onto his back, and he landed on a pile of deep snow. For a moment he blacked out.

When he regained consciousness, the firefighters had already moved on to another warehouse. Flames danced wildly from its rooftop.

Jussi and his crew positioned an enormous ladder against the side of the brick building. Aarne stood up, brushed the snow from his jacket, and ran over to assist.

"OK, boys," said Jussi. "Get that hose into the top of the roof. We can soak the fire from above and maybe save this one."

"What can I do, Isä?" Aarne asked.

"You climb up, and let me know when everyone is ready to go. That hose has to be in the right place before we start, or it will be too difficult to control."

Aarne nodded. He climbed the rungs one by one. The higher he went, the more intense was the heat. The men hauled the heavy hose up the building and placed it in the roof. If they could attack the inferno from above, they might be able to douse the flames. Maybe they wouldn't save the building, but they might be able to stop the sparks from spreading.

Aarne tried to shout over the intense sounds of the raging flames and the clamour of human activity below.

"Turn it on," he called to his father on the ground, motioning to release the valve.

Jussi nodded and gave his team the order.

Water gushed through the hose, making it twist and turn like a giant snake. The men struggled to keep their balance. Aarne held on with all his might. As the water surged, the hose nearly knocked him off the ladder. He held steady, hoping the building would remain standing.

A thin sheet of ice soon coated the ladder's rungs. Aarne was soaked. His clothes froze in the frigid air. The men had drenched the flames and saved the building. They exchanged smiles but soon were back to work. Aarne felt a wave of relief and pride.

Step by step he tried to lower himself down, but his clothes were frozen solid. He gripped the ladder with his icy fingers as his feet slipped on the rungs. Finally he reached the ground, teeth chattering as he watched the steam rise from the soaked warehouse.

"Better get warmed up, Aarne," his father said, nodding in approval. "You did good work here."

Aarne smiled. He looked for Kalle, hoping he'd be ready to go home.

Aarne and Kalle left the scene behind, passing the Ainola kindergarten, its main building nearly destroyed. Nearby, on the other side of the bridge from Åström Park, a Russian bomb had hit the sidewalk in front of the girls' school, which the boys had nicknamed the *tipala* because of the tipa, tipa, tipa sounds little birds made. The boys often joked that the girls were the little birds, but Aarne didn't feel like joking now.

A blast had carved a huge hole in the middle of the park. Water covered everything. Walls of buildings were caving in, and electric cables were stretching so far that sparks flew. The suffocating smell of smoke filled the air.

Aarne and Kalle went home briefly, but were soon compelled to return to the areas of devastation. They helped a man pull his possessions from his burning shed and a family carry furniture from their house. When the blare of sirens returned, they ducked under the street into the culvert for protection. They huddled breathlessly for a few terrifying moments until the sounds ceased.

As they emerged, Aarne noticed a fire had broken out in the courtyard of Hotel Arina. A family who lived nearby on Pakahuone Street were hauling their belongings into the street. He watched as a young girl tried to shift a large, wooden dresser by herself. As she struggled a drawer fell out, scattering its contents across the snow.

"Can I help you with that?" Aarne asked the girl.

"*Kiitos.* Thank you," she said as she picked up a pile of papers.

She looked up at Aarne with a smile. The brightness of her blue eyes startled him. He smiled back. Laughing, the two tried to capture the papers as they scattered in the breeze.

Aarne noticed the dog-eared edge of a photograph peeking from a pile of snow. He picked it up, wiped off the flakes, and turned to the girl, intending to return it to her. He paused to look at her picture. She was the prettiest girl he had ever seen. Hoping she didn't notice, he slipped the photograph into his coat pocket. When they had gathered the entire drawer's contents, Aarne and the girl stood together, staring.

Finally she spoke. "Thank you for helping me."

Her voice was quiet. She smiled, barely able to meet his gaze. Aarne was about to ask her name, but before he could she turned and walked in the direction of her house. Aarne watched her move away, wondering if he would ever see her again.

Instead of heading for home, Aarne decided to walk over to Iso Katu, to look at his former neighbourhood and his first house. His was one of many wooden houses attached side by side in a townhouse style that lined the main street of Oulu.

When Aarne arrived, Uncle Yrjo, Jussi's brother, was already there, gauging the damage. The entire block was devastated. Bombs had torn holes into the row of houses, and rubble was scattered across the street.

Uncle Yrjo looked up as Aarne approached.

"Hell of a mess," Uncle Yrjo said, shaking his head. "But I don't think I'll die in this war yet."

Aarne surveyed the charred remains of his previous home. He vaguely remembered living here, at 48 Iso Katu. Jussi and Anna Liisa, with their three older children, Heimo, Veikko and Lylli, along with their youngest, Kalle and Aarne, had lived in three small rooms. Aarne remembered a wood stove in the corner heating the house. His mother had cooked simple meals in the small kitchen, and on Sundays she'd often put on a pot roast with vegetables and kept it in the oven all day, so a warm meal would be ready for the famished boys when they returned from skiing or other pursuits. Aarne recalled it was an active and happy household, with the children constantly busy. As in their other homes, the neighbourhood youngsters were always welcome, and the house brimmed with the noise of children.

Now only its ashes remained.

Aarne looked at the stoic face of his uncle before turning his attention back to the devastation before him. The two stood side by side, the man and the boy, arms crossed, watching the steam rise from the ashes and dissipate into the air.

—⚌—

It was a long winter. News arrived that Heimo had been injured and sent to Sweden to recover. Aarne waited with anticipation for his brother's return. By mid-March, the 105 days of war had ended. Finland's small army and aged weaponry were ultimately no match for Russia's more powerful artillery and greater man power. Despite the defeat Aarne and his family were relieved that Heimo would soon be coming home.

In the meantime Kalle found a job hauling wood for the hyrdoelectric power plant. With a shortage of able-bodied men, it was not uncommon to find youths working jobs formerly held by older men.

One day, as Aarne was waiting for his brother's shift to end, he overheard a conversation between the foreman and Kalle.

"What do you think, Kalle? Will Aarne work for us?" the man asked.

"Why don't you ask him yourself?" Kalle replied.

"Where is he?"

"He's there, sitting in the sandbox." Kalle laughed as he pointed towards Aarne, waiting nearby.

Although he was just a boy, Aarne readily accepted the job. From that day on, he rose in the early hours of the morning and joined the other workers. The wood-powered trucks had to be pushed out of the garage and down the slanted floor, so they could be started outside; otherwise the fumes from the gas would harm everyone inside. Once the vehicles were ready, Aarne stacked the wood on the trucks and delivered them to the power plant, making two or three trips each day to ensure a steady supply for producing the steam power that generated electricity for the city.

At the end of the day, around five or six o'clock, Aarne returned home.

"Why don't you rest?" Anna Liisa asked him. "You must be so exhausted."

"I'm all right, Äiti."

He cleaned up and had a quick meal and then headed to town for a few hours of entertainment, eager to spend some of his newly earned money. Although no longer feeling like a child, Aarne enjoyed this relatively peaceful period after the Finnish-Russian war, despite the conflict that continued to rage through Europe.

The work was hard, but Aarne never complained. He wanted to prove he was a strong, capable worker. He was determined to be as good as any of the older men around him. There was no time for being a teenager during the war. One was a child; then one was not.

—∞—

Several months after the war ended, Heimo finally returned home after convalescing in Sweden. Aarne had waited impatiently for his return and was overjoyed to see him, although as they embraced he noticed his older brother looked paler and thinner than he remembered.

The family gathered around Heimo in the small living room, his mother fussing to find him a comfortable chair and his father looking on with concern. During the war, Aarne knew, Heimo had spent most of the time in the north, fighting the Russians on the border.

"Tell us what happened, Heimo. How did you get hurt?" Aarne asked.

His mother gave him a sharp look. "Let your brother rest," she said. "There will be plenty of time to talk to him about that later." She poured Heimo a hot drink and passed it to him.

"It's all right, Äiti," Heimo said. "I can talk about it." He propped himself on his pillow and took a sip of the coffee. "Well, we were out there on the border. It was a freezing day. The fighting was getting really fierce, and the Russians seemed to be pretty close by. I don't know what was worse—the Russians or the weather. It happened so quickly, it's hard to remember."

Aarne waited as Heimo took a sip. He leaned in closer as he watched his older brother.

"There was a lot of gunfire and explosions in every direction. It was hard to see the enemy, but you knew they were right there in front of you. Before I knew it, from out of nowhere something hit me. It felt like my leg exploded. I fell over in pain."

"Then what happened?" Aarne asked.

"Then I don't know. I saw the blood soaking into the snow around me. I couldn't move. I tried to stay conscious, but I think I passed out. Someone must have moved me because I woke up in one of the tents with the other injured soldiers. They said I had to wait. The fighting was too intense, so it wasn't safe to evacuate the wounded right away. Someone had packed snow around my leg. It was numb."

Aarne couldn't take his eyes off his brother. He wanted to see the leg but was too afraid to ask.

"When the fighting slowed down," Heimo continued, "they carried me onto a truck and finally transported us to a military hospital in a nearby town. The doctor tried to save my leg, but it was too damaged, so he had to amputate." He motioned to a place just below his knee.

Aarne looked at him with concern.

"Don't worry. Can't feel a thing." Heimo pulled up his pants, revealing his wooden leg. He smiled at Aarne. "Good as new," he said, knocking on the leg with his knuckles. "I'm ready to go dancing."

"What happened at the hospital? I heard there was an attack," Anna Liisa said.

"We must have been there for several days by then, and I was recovering pretty well from the surgery. But then the hospital was bombed. Can you believe it? We're in the hospital, and they bomb us again." Heimo shook his head in disbelief. "The hospital staff managed to get most of the wounded out. But not everyone made it. I may have lost my leg, but others weren't so fortunate."

Aarne nodded, admiring his brother's positive attitude despite his circumstances. It felt good to have him home again.

—◠◠◠—

On Aarne's thirteenth birthday in early June, he and Kalle decided to ride their bicycles to one of their favourite beaches. The lake was crystal clear, and the sandy beach sparkled in the early summer sunshine. It was a small enough body of water that it warmed up earlier than the other lakes. The boys spent several hours swimming and diving, splashing and laughing, like carefree children again.

When their afternoon of freedom came to a close, Aarne and Kalle packed up their belongings and headed home, the warm sun and breeze drying them as they rode.

"What's that up there?" Kalle asked. They slowed their bicycles.

"I...I don't know," Aarne said. He stopped his bike beside Kalle's.

In the harbour he saw a large ship gleaming against the waves. Military tents were set up in a wide-open area, colourful items were hanging from tree branches, and several boats were stationed in the harbour, loaded with mountains of hay for horses. Soldiers in official Nazi uniforms looked like they were preparing for business.

The Germans had arrived.

Aarne and Kalle looked at each other in astonishment. They had never seen so many soldiers in one place before. They got on their bikes and pedaled as fast as they could, eager to tell their family what they had seen.

The German soldiers created housing for themselves in an area the citizens soon dubbed Small Berlin. Those who lived nearby swore they could hear the sounds of gunfire from the area at all times of the day and night. Some believed the Germans were target shooting while others feared that civilians were being shot. It took no time for the people of Oulu, including Aarne, to feel the Germans' presence and to fear them.

One day shortly after the influx of the German military, Aarne heard a story about a young man walking in the town with his girlfriend. A German soldier approached them; he seemed to want to talk to the attractive, young woman. The couple wanted nothing to do with the soldier, and the two men began to argue. Within a few short minutes, the German soldier shot the Finnish man right there on the street, leaving the girl screaming in terror. It didn't take long for the story to spread through the town. Aarne's unease continued to grow.

Fifteen days after Aarne's birthday, Finland's war with Russia resumed. Finland was allied with Germany. Oulu was now a garrison town. Life was about to change for Aarne again.

—∿—

Aarne and Kalle continued working as the Continuation War raged on into the winter of 1942. Heimo was learning to adapt to his amputation. This time Aarne's brother, Veikko, had enlisted and was fighting the Russians as part of a Finnish skiing military unit that travelled and fought using their cross-country skis, cloaked in white to blend with the winter terrain.

Aarne often lay awake in bed, worrying about his brother at the front. He knew Veikko was well suited for this assignment. His brother had always been an exceptional skier. Veikko had once told Aarne about the time he had won a ski race at school and received a fresh orange as a prize. Veikko had never tasted or even seen an orange before. He took a giant bite out of the dimpled fruit, peel and all, and immediately spit out the sour, leathery skin.

"What did you do?" Aarne had asked, laughing at his brother's reaction.

"I was so angry, I threw the orange against a shed behind the school. Only problem was a few of the girls saw me and told the teacher. She came out, hopping mad, and made me stand in the corner for the rest of the day." Veikko had smiled at the memory.

Aarne remembered another time when Anna Liisa had forbidden Veikko from attending school because he was running a high fever. Aarne had felt sorry for him that day because he was supposed to be skiing in a race.

Veikko pleaded with his mother, but Anna Liisa had forced him back to bed. Aarne left for school but learned later that when his mother was busy, Veikko snuck out of the house and ran to school. His father went to deliver the sick boy home, but by the time he arrived Veikko, sweating and feverish, had already finished and won the race.

Aarne was concerned about his brother but knew his skiing ability was unmatched. He believed Veikko would return home safely and, he hoped, in one piece.

One day Aarne returned home after a short time away. Veikko, he learned from Lylli, had fallen violently ill while skiing in subarctic temperatures on the Russian border. He went to the hospital where he was treated for pneumonia, a common ailment amongst the Finnish ski troopers.

"How is he?" Aarne asked. "Can I see him?" It had been so long since he had seen his older brother.

"Veikko was discharged from the hospital and went home to his wife, Aune, and their baby, Seppo. He was so happy to hold his eight-month-old son for the first time." Lylli's eyes filled with tears. "While holding Seppo, he began coughing and vomiting blood. His strength failed. Aarne, he died."

Aarne stared at his sister in disbelief. Grief overcame him.

Chapter 3
Helsinki, 1943

—∿—

"I want to go to Helsinki," Aarne said, a slight waver in his voice.

Anna Liisa turned from her cooking, wiping her hands on her long, chequered apron. His father stopped reading, a cup of coffee steaming beside him, and placed the newspaper on the wooden table before him. He paused. His parents looked at him in disbelief.

"I'm going to find work there." He fiddled with the small piece of paper he had twisted in a tight cone shape between his fingers. At fifteen he was too young to be in the army or even train for the military, and his hometown was teeming with soldiers of the Third Reich. He saw no reason to stay.

"I'm ready to leave home." Aarne shuffled his feet as he waited for a reaction. His brother, Heimo, had already served in the military, losing a limb in the process. Veikko had died as a result of fighting the Russians in Northern Finland, and Kalle was in military training in Helsinki. His sister, Lylli, was married and living nearby. He was the only son still living under their roof.

Aarne noticed his mother and father glancing at each other before turning their attention back to him.

"No, you are too young." Jussi's voice was stern and decisive.

"I'm old enough. I can take care of myself." Aarne crossed his arms. He refused to let his father sway him.

"What are you going to do there? You're just a boy," his mother said. She wrung her hands in her dirty dishtowel.

"I'll find a job. I already have work here, so I'm sure someone will hire me. There's a shortage of men, Äiti. They need strong, young people like me."

"You should stay here with us. It's too dangerous in the big city, and you'll be far away from your family."

Aarne could see the tight lines around his mother's mouth and a deep crease form between her eyes. He had seen that expression many times before when she had pleaded with him to avoid the dangerous river rapids of the Oulujoki. But he could never be deterred.

Aarne had always loved the nearby Ainola Park and the many bridges, streams, and creeks. It was an idyllic place, with tall, green trees swaying in the wind, gurgling water trickling over rocks under white wooden footbridges, and the ever present clamour of the powerful Oulujoki as it raced to the sea. Aarne and Matti, along with their friend, Erkki, spent the summer roving around the park and the river, finding mischief wherever they could.

Despite his mother's warnings, he could not avoid its temptations. The Oulujoki snaked through the town from outlying farms and forests. Many merchants used the river to transport wood, tar, and salmon to the harbour to be shipped all over the world. It was also a favourite place for fishermen and swimmers. Even the women washed their clothes in the water, heating their laundry in large cauldrons by the shore and hanging it on tree branches for the breeze to dry while their children played on the rocks. At times the river was quiet and gentle, the currents moving strongly below the surface. At other times it was noisy and powerful, sprays of water dancing over the protruding rocks. To Aarne it was an ideal playground.

For fun Aarne, Matti, and Erkki would drop a plank into the fast flowing water to watch it jumping and skipping, turning and twisting with the currents as it headed towards the powerhouse's turnpikes. When they tired of watching the wood pieces, they walked upriver, stripped their clothes, and left them hanging on the side of the riverbank. They jumped into the icy water, letting it pull them through the currents, feet stuck up in front, bottoms hitting the rocks below, and hands trying to navigate away from the giant turbines towards a safer channel. What a thrill it was to ride the rapids, danger looming up ahead, threatening to dismember them if they made a wrong move. Brief moments of panic turned into roars of relief as they manoeuvred away from the monstrous turbines into a safer, more peaceful canal.

Now Aarne eyed his mother's worried expression. His father's face was emotionless.

"I'm going even if I don't have your permission," Aarne said, the resolve written in the set of his jaw and the flash of his blue eyes.

Anna Liisa sighed. Jussi picked up his paper.

"Better get packing, son," his father said.

Aarne beamed.

—⟩⟩⟨⟨—

On the day of Aarne's travel to Helsinki, he organized his few belongings, combed back his hair, and shined his shoes. Anna Liisa was in the kitchen, preparing food for his journey.

"Don't make anything for me," he said. "I don't need it."

She ignored him, her back turned away as she focused her attention on slicing a loaf of home-cooked rye bread.

"You'll need it later," she said in her quiet, resolute voice.

"I'll be fine, Äiti."

Anna Liisa turned to face him. She smiled, but he could see the tears forming at the corners of her eyes. "Maybe so, but take them anyway. You may change your mind later."

She handed him the carefully wrapped sandwiches.

"And you don't need to come with me to the railroad station," Aarne said, reluctantly accepting his mother's parting gift and placing them in his bag. "I'm not a child anymore. I don't need anyone's help."

Anna Liisa gave him a long embrace.

"Be safe, my son," she said. "Don't forget your home."

Aarne tightened his grip around his petite mother and then turned to shake hands with his father.

"Goodbye, Isä," Aarne said.

Jussi nodded, his face composed, but held his son's hand in his strong grip a little longer than usual.

Aarne walked to the Oulu railway station alone.

When he arrived he realized he was too early for the train to Helsinki. He paid his fare and sat on a wooden bench to wait. His leg twitched up and down as he fidgeted with the ticket between his thumb and forefinger. Every so often he glanced up at the station's clock, slowly ticking away the endless minutes before the train would arrive. It felt like an eternity. His stomach lurched, tossing and turning like the rapids against the rocks of the Oulujoki.

One by one Aarne removed the sandwiches from the brown paper bag and unwrapped them carefully. The rye bread was fresh and moist, with the delicious fragrance of his mother's kitchen. He observed the clock, still ticking along. Aarne gulped the sandwiches down, barely chewing, as his mind wandered.

He thought of his grandfather, Wilhelm Kovala, a respected entrepreneur who had owned several businesses in Oulu. Wilhelm had owned a hardware store where, amongst other things, he sold bicycles. He boasted the distinction of having sold the very first automobile in Oulu, to one of the owners of the Åström Brothers leather factory. Wilhelm also had a local movie theatre, where his son, Jussi, and oldest grandsons once worked. As a young girl Lylli used to deliver their meals in the evening, stopping to peer at the films through the small windows of the projection room. Aarne wondered if her teeth marks were still embedded in the windowsill where she clenched down during the scary parts. His thoughts turned to his father, whose first job was sharpening blades at the local sawmill. Later he worked as a fireman for the railroad, shovelling coal into the engine's firebox. Now Jussi made a good living as the head mechanic for the hydrolectric plant.

Aarne wondered what kind of job he would find in Helsinki. Would he be an entrepreneur like his grandfather? Or would he be like his father, working with his hands? The whole world with its infinite possibilities seemed to spread before him.

As the train pulled into the station, wind gusts signalling its arrival, the screeching of the brakes woke Aarne from his reverie. He grabbed his bag and stood at the platform's edge, like a soldier at attention, his ticket bent and crumpled in his hand. A few others had arrived, handing bags and children up to the passenger cars. An older couple embraced a young man and woman before they entered the train, waving and blowing kisses. Was the young man off to war? Aarne wondered.

Aarne stepped off the platform and onto the train. He found a seat by the window overlooking the station. He watched as family and friends outside smiled and waved at the other passengers. No one stood on the platform to wave good-bye to him.

He turned away and stared straight ahead, waiting for the journey to begin. After several long minutes, the whistle blew. With a jolt the train dragged itself away from the station. Steam briefly obscured his view as the sound of the engines filled the compartment. He took one last look through the window as his hometown faded in the distance.

—m—

When the train arrived in Helsinki's central train station, Aarne felt a strange nervousness reawakening in the pit of his stomach. He paused to look up at the impressive building, clad in granite, its clock tower soaring above, making him feel insignificant. Two pairs of hulky statues holding spheres on either side of the arched entranceway gazed across the street with impassive expressions. He was alone. Far from his parents. Far from home.

Aarne swung his bag across his shoulders and wandered from the station, looking for the street where his father's sister, Jenni Kovala, lived. Aunt Jenni's apartment was only a block away from Mannerheimintie, Helsinki's main street, renamed after the Winter War for the statesman and military leader Mannerheim. She lived in a little flat above a small grocery, where she also worked, in a tall brick building. When Aarne arrived at her door, she welcomed him warmly.

"Aarne, how tall you've grown." She smiled as she helped him with his bag. "How are your parents?"

"Everyone's well," Aarne said as he hung his coat on the hook and removed his shoes. He told her about his brothers and sister as she prepared a simple meal of rye bread and *hernekeitto*, or pea soup, and a dessert of baked pulla, along with hot coffee made with the grounds from a previous pot. Sugar was a luxury rarely found.

"It's difficult everywhere," Aunt Jenni said. "Helsinki has been bombed several times. There has been much damage to the buildings and lots of injuries. Several deaths as well." Aunt Jenni shook her head. "Life is not easy, Aarne. We have to make the best of things."

Aarne agreed. He thought of his father fighting fires after the bombings during the Winter War, his first home on Iso Katu destroyed. He remembered his mother standing in long lines with her food stamps and bicycling to local farms to trade for produce. He considered Heimo, struggling to adjust to the loss of his leg. Veikko's wife and child were left without a husband and a father. Kalle was preparing to join the war efforts. He knew he could no longer be idle at home. His future seemed so uncertain. Would he able to make the best of things?

After their meal Aunt Jenni gave Aarne directions to the market, suggesting he walk down Mannerheimintie through the Esplanadi Park until he reached the *kauppatori*, or market square.

Aarne strolled past the stately brick buildings, looking up at the interesting architecture and the tall trees lining the street. It was such a big and busy city compared to Oulu.

The long street opened before him to reveal a market on the harbour front. The action of the kauppatori, filled with the hustle and bustle of market activity, invigorated him. Women passed to and fro with their packages while vendors called out the day's deals. Sailors from the nearby ships stopped by the stalls and shouted to one another on their way to the town. Young men in military uniforms hurled insults and pushed one another playfully.

The odour of fish floated through the air from fishermen's boats tied in the harbour, where they sold their day's catch. A stall with felt boots, jackets and hats of red, blue, and yellow provided a burst of colour against the grey blue of the Baltic Sea and the worn cobblestones of the market square. One stall displayed knives and kitchen tools along with jewellery and other goods made of the smooth, white antlers of reindeer. Above, seagulls squawked and dove for bits of fallen food. The day was grey and chilly, but the market was alive with colours and fragrances.

As Aarne strolled past the stalls, he inhaled the sweet scent of the pulla's cardamom and the steam rising from the *riisipiirakkat*, rye pastries filled with rice and topped with melting butter, reminding him of Hukanen's bakery, owned by his father's cousin, and making his mouth water with the memory of sweet treats.

As a child Aarne had often assisted the deliveryman by sitting on his cart as he delivered baked goods from the bakery to various stores around town. His version of helping mainly consisted of adding more weight to the cart. The driver didn't seem to mind, however. He frequently gave Aarne a ride, and the two chatted together along the route. Sometimes Aarne and his brothers worked in the bakery itself, keeping the fire stoked or sweeping up, and were rewarded with soft, chewy gingerbreads or little fruit cakes. Aarne loved the jelly-filled donuts covered in sugar best of all. Now his mouth watered as the bakery smells drifted from the market stall.

Aarne wandered through the lively marketplace. What was he going to do here in the capital? Had he made the right decision? He knew his stubbornness sometimes led to rash decisions. His brothers and sisters often teased him about being so obstinate. But once he had his mind made up, there was no stopping him. He had contemplated this decision for a long time. And now here he was.

"*Hei*, Aarne. What are you doing in Helsinki?"

Aarne recognized a young man and a couple of boys from Oulu waving at him. He waved back and crossed the square to meet them.

"Looking for work. I've only just arrived from Oulu," Aarne explained, happy to see familiar faces in this hurried city. "What about you?"

"Training to fight, of course, just like your brother," the young man replied. "Have you seen him?"

"Kalle? Not yet, but I'm hoping to soon. Do you know how I can contact him?"

"I heard he was stationed at an island called Santahamina," the young man said. "But he'll need to ask permission to see you. He can't just leave without making a request. It could take a long time."

"I understand," Aarne said, looking downcast. "I guess I shouldn't have expected to see him right away."

Seeing Aarne's disappointment, the young man said, "Don't worry. I'm sure it will work out, and you'll see him soon. We'll try to get word to him for you."

"Kiitos." Aarne wasn't so convinced. All of a sudden, he felt a familiar hollowness filling his belly. Homesickness replaced his earlier nerves.

—⚭—

To Aarne's surprise, the next day Kalle contacted Aunt Jenni and made arrangements to meet in Helsinki. Aunt Jenni explained that his friends from Oulu had managed to get a message to Kalle, and his superiors had granted him permission for a few hours' leave.

Aarne waited eagerly all day. When the time finally arrived, he flew out of Aunt Jenni's apartment and down the street to the meeting place, a small restaurant on the main street.

"Kalle, I'm so happy to see you, brother." Aarne smiled widely at his sibling.

Kalle grinned as he stood up from the table and shook hands with him. Aarne pulled off his jacket and hung it against the back of his chair. After ordering, they spoke briefly about home and Kalle's experiences in the army.

"So what are your plans?" Kalle asked.

They sat together like old times, both as comfortable as if they hadn't been apart these many months.

"I'm not sure yet. Aunt Jenni is letting me stay with her until I can find work and a place. Do you have any ideas about what I could do?" Aarne was eager to discuss his future with Kalle. It had been a long time since he could share anything with his brother.

"You might try at one of the shops or factories. There are also some ships that come into the harbour. They need men, I think. But it's dangerous work. You might be safer staying in Helsinki."

Aarne thought about it. "I'll just have to see what comes up, I guess. But working on a ship would be perfect."

The two continued talking for several hours. Aarne wished Kalle could stay all evening, but soon Kalle announced that he was expected back at Santahamina. Outside they shook hands and promised to meet again soon. They parted, turning in different directions down the street. Aarne wondered when that time would come.

—⁂—

A few days after his reunion with Kalle, Aarne learned of a merchant marine ship docked in the harbour. He had always dreamed of being a sailor. As a child he had marvelled at the big ships in Oulu's harbour. When the ships came to dock, he, Kalle and the neighbourhood boys would run to meet them, hoping to beat the other children who also wanted to trade beautifully ornate matchstick boxes with the sailors.

All of the children had collections. Aarne's friend, Esko Mustonen, had one of the largest matchbox collections he had ever seen. He even boasted he had the biggest collection in the world. Esko lived across the street from the Kovalas' house. He was an aspiring entertainer and used his sizeable yard as a stage on which he directed the neighbourhood boys in original plays. The yard was crisscrossed by clotheslines on which hung freshly laundered sheets, strategically placed to create the walls of the stage. Aarne spent many happy hours pretending to be an actor on Esko's stage. Years later Esko would train to be an actor and have a popular national radio show. Until then, when he wasn't acting or directing, Esko collected matchstick boxes with the other children. To them the traded items were little treasures from faraway places. Besides, it gave the boys a chance to talk to the sailors and find out where they had been.

Aarne had admired the men working on the boats and wondered what life would be like aboard one of the massive vessels. He imagined being at the wheel, steering through busy harbours and across vast oceans. As the ships set sail, Aarne would watch them from the pier until the smoke disappeared on the distant horizon, hoping someday he would be the one steering a ship to some exotic destination. Now he had his chance. He would enquire about a job aboard the S/S *Wappu*.

The next day he decided to see the ship for himself. He said goodbye to Aunt Jenni and made his way to the harbour, taking a now familiar route. As he crossed the marketplace, Aarne was in awe of the size of the vessel.

He looked around for someone who might be in charge. Everyone seemed to be in a hurry. In the distance, he heard a man yelling orders at the crew who rushed about transporting cargo to and from the boat. Aarne approached him.

"Excuse me, sir. I'm looking for work. Are there any jobs on the ship?" Aarne asked in his most determined voice.

The man paused from his work to look over the young man. "How old are you, boy?"

"Sixteen," Aarne said, hoping his lie did not show on his face. He was fifteen, but his height and size might help him pass for an older boy.

"Well, there is work, but if you aren't old enough you need a letter of permission from your parents. Where are they?"

"They're in Oulu. I don't have such a letter and didn't know I would need one. Besides, I'm already here, and I want to work."

Aarne pulled back his shoulders and straightened his spine. He stood with his feet planted firmly on the ground and looked the seasoned sailor squarely in the eyes. Between his thumb and forefinger, he twisted the fabric at the edge of his woolen coat in his nervous fashion.

Aarne was tall and thin but muscular. His large, calloused hands suggested he was used to hard work. He counted on the fact that so many Finnish men were fighting in the war while others were training to fight. The scarcity of able sailors gave this man little choice but to hire him.

Aarne waited for his response. "My parents know I'm in Helsinki, and they know I'm looking for work. They'd support me taking this job."

"*Hyvää.* Good. We need men, but you have to be willing to work hard. The ship is no place for boys," the man said. "With this war going on, you need nerves of steel."

"Kiitos," Aarne replied. "You won't regret this. I'm a good worker, and I learn fast."

Finally he had his chance. He would be a sailor.

Chapter 4
S/S *Wappu*, 1943–1944

—∿—

Aarne's first night aboard the *Wappu* was not exactly what he had expected. He was nervous and excited about sailing from Helsinki to Hamburg and determined to make a good impression on his captain, Vihtori Jansen, and his shipmates.

When the crew gathered for mealtime, Aarne served himself and joined the sailors in the mess only to find the seats around the well-used wooden tables nearly filled. He tried to get a glimpse of the captain but soon learned that Jansen and the engineers ate their meals in a separate area, away from the regular crew. With his food in hand, Aarne noticed a spot beside a young sailor about his age.

"Anyone sitting here?" Aarne asked.

The young man shook his head, nodding to sit down as he chewed.

"Kiitos. Aarne," he said as he placed his food on the table and offered his hand.

"Kalevi. Pleased to meet you," the sailor said between bites, shaking Aarne's hand firmly.

The sounds of cutlery on plates and the chatter and laughter of the mariners made Aarne feel at ease.

"Where are you from, Aarne?" Kalevi asked before taking a big bite from his fork.

"Oulu. What about you?"

"Ylöjärvi, west of Tampere. I see you're new to the ship. I haven't been here too long either, but you'll get used to it. They sound tough, but they're good men."

Aarne looked around the table at the men, smiling and sharing jokes. Laughter emitted from the corner of the room. At another table two men were in deep debate, leaning over the table with looks of concentration. This was a family of sorts, he decided.

The aroma of the hot meal filled the air, and soon the company distracted him with their stories of the sea. It didn't take long before he took part in the discussions. He knew then that he belonged.

When the men had finished their meals, they picked up their cutlery, plates, and cups and brought them to the kitchen to wash them in large tubs of hot, soapy water. When Aarne's turn to take care of his dishes arrived, he entered the kitchen, looking for a place to put down his dinnerware. The water used for washing was filled with dirty suds, and food scraps floated on the surface. *I should replenish the water,* he thought. *It would be a nice thing to do for the rest of the crew.* With both hands he gripped the edge of the large, metal bucket and carried it to the deck, soapy water slopping from side to side, spilling over the edge as he walked. He swung the bucket back slightly, and with one great heave he threw the dirty contents over the side, into the ocean below.

To his astonishment the silverware sparkled and spun through the air until the forks, knives, and spoons plop, plop, plopped into the sea below.

For sure, he thought, *I'm going to be fired now.*

Aarne delivered the empty tub back to the kitchen, approaching the head cook, Papunen, with trepidation.

"I'm very sorry." Aarne tried to look the cook in the eyes, feeling his face flush. He explained what he had done.

Papunen glowered at the young sailor but held her tongue.

Aarne waited. He shuffled back and forth.

Finally she responded. "Don't worry, son. We can buy new cutlery when we arrive at port in Kotka."

Aarne exhaled. He looked up at the cook. Her face had softened, and she smiled at the new sailor. "We can make do until then."

On his first night, Aarne climbed into the top of one of the two-tiered bunks in the small sleeping quarters. He shared the cabin with three other sailors, making it difficult at times to move around. One was already sleeping soundly, his snores echoing against the bare walls. The others were on duty. The men had only a few personal effects—a photo or two from home, some books, or items acquired in various ports. Aarne didn't have anything to display, but he felt in his jacket pocket for the crumpled photograph of the girl with the dresser in the snow. He pinned the photograph near his bed, where he could see it before closing his eyes. Perhaps he would see her again someday.

After many nights Aarne would become accustomed to sleeping at sea. While the movement might gently rock him to sleep, it was also capable of throwing him violently from his bed. Even the most experienced sailors sometimes felt seasickness when the waves started tossing the ship like a plastic toy under the spout of a bathtub. On the first night, the vessel swayed back and forth in a constant, lulling motion. Aarne crossed his hands behind his head and let his heavy eyelids droop until the concerns of his first day were swept away, and he was dreaming of his friends and his beloved town.

Aarne envisioned Matti and Erkki pulling their little crafts up the river, rambling alongside the wild Oulujoki. They tied their boats to a tree at the river's edge and entered the cold water, feeling the rapids push against their legs and splash up against their faces. Aarne let the fast flowing river pull him through the water, his feet propped in front as he tried to avoid the jutting rocks. Using his hands and body to navigate across the expanse, he found himself in a little channel that brought him to the open sea. There he and the boys landed on Oulu's best beach and spent the whole day enjoying the sand and the sun. With a few *markkas* from his pocket, he bought a pop and ice cream from one of the stands.

When the day drew to a close, the boys walked across the island and jumped on the back of the ferry, hoping to hitch a ride to the marketplace at the edge of town. Once they crossed the worst part of the river, and not before, the kind ferryman pretended to notice them finally and kicked the boys off because they hadn't paid. The boys swam back the rest of the way.

Aarne smiled at the recollection. He dozed off.

The ship's steel interior made the nights extremely chilly. In the winter months, even the bunks were frosty, and Aarne's blanket sometimes froze to the wall. Now, when he woke in the morning, he could see his breath hanging in the air, and he shivered under his thin blanket. His thoughts wandered to his small house in Oulu, warm with the fire from the wood stove, the aroma of home cooking wafting through the house. The only thing he could smell in this small space was his mates' stale socks.

It took only a few days before Aarne learned the ship's routines. Molin, the head sailor, ordered him to do a variety of odd jobs. Most of the older crew worked in the engine room or were mechanics. The smaller jobs went to the young sailors. They usually worked in pairs; one steered the boat for two hours at a time while his mate did other work, like painting and scraping when out at open sea or searching for water mines in dangerous locations. Every two hours the two switched places. During these shifts he was often paired with his new friend, Kalevi.

The work was a continuous repetition of the same pattern: work four hours, rest four hours. His schedule continued for weeks on end with no break. There was little leisure time. By the time he ate and had a short sleep, he was back to work. He looked forward to docking in port when he would get a half-day leave onshore and rest from his exhausting schedule.

Aarne was no stranger to sea life. When he was a young boy, his family had lived in the Kuusiluoto neighbourhood of Oulu, in a wooden row house. His backyard was the gently rolling waves of the incredibly blue Baltic Sea, yet he was only steps away from the hustle of the town. A variety of family owned vessels lined the shore. The other children had small boats or canoes, but Aarne's boat had a motor, so they would often call upon him to tow them behind him. The boys loved to roam around the archipelago, and sometimes they met other boys and had little battles at sea with them, paddles flying high and water splashing everywhere. Now Aarne was faced with dangers on a grander scale.

One day he stood on deck, waiting for instructions to steer the ship. He had done so many times before but never in the Kiel Canal.

"Perhaps someone else should take the wheel," Molin suggested.

A few sailors looked at Aarne and then at each other. He wondered if they thought he wasn't up for the job. It required steady nerves. A wrong move could be disastrous.

Aarne looked from the head sailor to Captain Jansen.

"Go ahead and change," Jansen said. He crossed his arms and looked directly at Aarne.

"Yes, Captain."

Molin moved aside for Aarne while the others looked on with anticipation. Aarne could see a few glances exchanged, but nobody dared protest the captain's orders.

Without a word Aarne took the large steering wheel and planted his feet firmly shoulder width apart. He positioned his hands at ten and two o'clock, straightened his back, and squared his shoulders. Before him the compass directed his passage. If he was nervous, he wasn't going to let them see it.

From the corner of his eye, Aarne could see Captain Jansen looking on with his arms crossed. His face was expressionless. Aarne's crewmates were motionless.

Aarne steered. The Kiel Canal was ninety-eight kilometres in length, with locks at either end, linking the North Sea to the Baltic Sea in the German state of Schleswig-Holstein. The Germans were building warships in the cities along the Kiel, so the canal was constantly under attack. When merchant ships like the *Wappu* arrived, a guide navigated the ship through the water mines, and because their cargo included materials for the war effort, other German vessels often gave way.

When Aarne had safely navigated the boat through the canal, the men showed their relief audibly. Aarne beamed his big grin. The captain nodded and turned his attention to other matters. Aarne was relieved that his first time through the Kiel had been a success, and he knew he would be ready when they called on him to navigate in and out of the harbours. He had the captain's approval and the respect of his mates.

—m—

One night Aarne was stationed on deck while the *Wappu* waited to be guided throught the Kiel.

"When the signal is given, wake the crew, and follow the German convoy," a crew member said.

"Yes, sir," he replied, eager to comply. It was already late at night, the air cool and crew unusually quiet. Most of the sailors, including Captain Jansen, were sleeping soundly in their quarters.

Several hours passed. There was little movement in the sea below and less in the air above. Aarne struggled to keep his eyes open. He sat in a chair, trying to keep himself awake. After waiting for a few hours, he drifted off.

"Aarne, wake up," a sailor shouted across the deck.

"What's going on?" Aarne struggled out of the fogginess of sleep, pulling his heavy body from its slump.

"We've missed the signal, and the convoy has already left."

Aarne fumbled and found his way to his feet. "I'm sorry. I didn't see the sign. It must have come after I dozed off."

Familiar footsteps sounded down the corridor. Aarne stood at attention as he heard the captain approach.

Captain Jansen looked at the crew. His forehead furrowed, and his lips tightened. "No sense in waiting here. I'll take her through."

He stepped up to the wheel. Aarne looked on but remained silent. Clearly the captain wasn't willing to wait for the next escort. The ship was already behind schedule, and he'd have to explain why he wasn't meeting his deadlines in his log. *Besides, he had been through the canal so many times, he probably knows the markers by heart,* Aarne thought.

Surprised that the captain hadn't reprimanded him for his error, Aarne was grateful. He didn't want to make that mistake again.

After that night he was determined never to fall asleep on the job again.

—◊◊◊—

The months passed quickly as Aarne adjusted to life aboard the *Wappu*. His thoughts often turned to his family and how they were faring in Oulu. He had no contact with his parents and often wondered about his family, especially his brothers, Kalle and Heimo.

One afternoon, the sun high in the sky and the wind whipping across the Baltic, Aarne was painting on deck. It seemed to be a job with no end. The warm rays felt good, but the cool breeze made him shiver. The *Wappu* was transporting German diesel trucks through the Kiel Canal, and Aarne noticed a few German soldiers sitting in one of the vehicles, away from the wind, enjoying some leisure time. Sometimes he could hear their chatter and laughter, but mostly he just ignored them. The German soldiers were under strict instructions and mainly kept to themselves. The Finns did the same.

As he made his long strokes against the rails, Aarne could hear the truck's engine sputter and start. He looked up to see the soldiers' panicked expressions. The engine continued to hum.

Other Finnish sailors on deck turned to see what was happening.

"Quick, help me. I can't turn it off," a soldier said, his eyes wide, desperately looking from one man to the next.

"I'll get a wrench from the engine room." A second soldier jumped down from the truck and hurried away. Aarne watched him rush past.

The Germans continued to fumble with the controls. They were clearly nervous now. Between applying strokes of paint, Aarne glanced up at them with curiosity. What kind of fools would turn on a truck on a ship in the middle of the canal?

"Sabotage, sabotage!" A German soldier pointed across the deck at the Finnish sailors.

The Finns looked at each other in disbelief. A few shook their heads and turned their backs to continue their duties. *We have nothing to do with this mess*, Aarne thought.

A few more minutes passed, with the Germans getting angrier and the Finns more amused. Finally one of the German soldiers managed to turn off the truck. Aarne could see their relief and embarrassment. With the show over, he turned back to his painting, leaving the soldiers to their truck.

—〰—

Despite the occasional tension between the Finns and the Germans aboard the *Wappu*, Aarne understood that their survival depended on the German antiaircraft gunners. He had seen planes shot down near the *Wappu*, explosions sending shrapnel everywhere, sometimes hitting other planes in the vicinity. The wreckage of an airplane rained down like thousands of bullets and caused the crew to fly for cover. Sometimes, during heavy fighting, Aarne positioned himself along the deck so he could jump into the sea. He hoped he would never have to evacuate the boat, but the alternative was less appealing.

One afternoon, as Aarne worked on deck, he heard the sounds of a low-flying airplane. He scanned the skies.

"What's going on?" he asked Kalevi, who was working nearby.

"Looks like that one's in trouble," he replied. "Russian, I think."

"Headed towards Sweden, I bet." Sweden was neutral territory. It was better for a plane to go down there than risk falling into enemy hands in Germany or elsewhere.

Aarne and Kalevi stopped working to watch the doomed aircraft. Suddenly its angle shifted. It was headed straight towards the *Wappu*.

Aarne froze in place.

The sailors on deck watched helplessly. The plane descended lower and lower, its nose pointed directly at them. Aarne considered bailing, but it would be of no use. If the plane hit, the *Wappu* would explode like a gigantic firecracker in the sea.

Aarne held his breath.

It was a clear, blue day, and the water lapped against the sides of the ship. The plane glided closer and closer as the sputtering sounds of its dying engines filled the air. This was it.

Aarne gripped the railing with white knuckles.

At the last moment, the pilot angled the aircraft away from the *Wappu*. It hit the sea and disappeared. A huge swell emerged from the calm surface, hammering the ship. Aarne held on to the side of the vessel, anchoring his feet for the impact. He looked in the direction of the plane's descent. There was no trace of it. The sea looked peaceful again, as though the aircraft and its inhabitants had never been there at all.

With shaking hands Aarne turned his attention back to his work, pausing for only a moment to look out across the Baltic Sea in the direction of his homeland.

—∾—

"Happy birthday, Aarne." The men raised their glasses.

"Kiitos." He grinned. It was June 10, 1944, his sixteenth birthday, and Aarne was celebrating with his friends in Lübeck, one of Germany's major port towns. The bar was bursting with patrons raising their glasses to one another. Aarne glanced at the faces of his shipmates. They looked older than when he had started, but he expected the work and the war had done the same to him.

The sailors enjoyed the evening, singing and drinking, but were startled when a sudden hush fell over the patrons.

"Turn it up." A loud German voice boomed across the room.

The bartender reached behind him, to a radio on a shelf. The distinctive voice of the leader of the Third Reich rumbled across the airwaves. Hitler reassured his listeners that although the Allies had arrived in Normandy only days before, on June 6, once they delivered all of their war materials to land the Germans would push them back into the sea. The crowd in the bar cheered. The Finnish sailors looked at one another sceptically.

By sixteen Aarne had already experienced war for a third of his young life. From the age of eleven, he had become familiar with the sounds of gunfire, grenades, bombs, and aircraft overhead. He had witnessed the destruction created by firebombs dropped on his hometown. He had seen planes shot down above him and ships sink into the sea below. Whole towns had been left in ruin and people's lives devastated. He thought he had seen all the desolation war could bring.

But he was wrong.

Several weeks after Aarne's birthday, the *Wappu* docked in the Finnish city of Kotka, close to the Russian border. It was a town Aarne and his crewmates had come to know quite well. When given a chance, they would leave the boat for a few hours to meander around the town, to eat, drink, and relax. That was when the town wasn't being bombed. Aarne was familiar with the large bomb shelter that was dug into a hillside near the harbour. Unlike other ports, where they were reserved for the citizens, Kotka's was available to anyone in the harbour area.

This time, as the sailors disembarked, news greeted them. A German antiaircraft cruiser, the *Niobe*, was stationed in Kotka in order to defend the port against Russian attack. About a week before, on July 16, 132 Russian bombers and fighters attacked the *Niobe*, probably mistaking it for the Finnish ship *Väinämöinen*, a battleship of a similar size. The *Niobe* retaliated, but the Russians devastated her in just eleven minutes. The vessel tipped and sank.

Knowing there were men aboard, several Finns from the town tried to help the crew, using their own boats to pick the stranded out of the water one by one. They rescued 260 people. For several days after, the citizens could still hear the sounds of banging from the interior of the hull, but they couldn't find any access into the damaged vessel. The citizens of Kotka tried desperately to cut through the boat to rescue the survivors, knowing that the men within the bowels of the torpedoed ship would surely die, but to no avail. Sixty of the *Niobe*'s crew members perished.

The news haunted Aarne. The fate of the *Niobe* made the dangers of his work during wartime a tangible reality, the evidence a hulking shell crippled in the harbour.

Several weeks later Aarne and Kalevi were in Hamburg. They were settling into a ferryboat ride from the port where the *Wappu* was docked, through the canals to the town center, when the familiar sounds of bombers infiltrated the skies above the city.

Hamburg was one of the busiest harbours in Europe and was under constant threat. The Americans and British pummelled the city every day and night, leaving its people half crazed from fear and sleeplessness. The devastation to the city made it barely recognizable.

Bomb shelters were available for the citizens, but visiting sailors needed a number to get into the protected areas. Despite the threat of attack, the captain allowed the sailors to go on shore leave, but they were on their own to find refuge if bombings took place during their stay.

Aarne scanned the sky above. It didn't look good.

"Better take cover," the ferry captain said, steering the boat from the open water into one of the canals. It was already too far from the port's bomb shelter to turn back and was still some distance from the town. Aarne wondered where they could possibly hide. Everyone watched the sky, wondering what the ferry captain would do.

"Not really anywhere safe out here," Kalevi said. "We're pretty exposed."

Aarne agreed. "Hopefully it'll be over quickly." He glanced up to see a group of planes flying in formation.

The ferry anchored close to a large building protruding out of the water. Against the red brick wall, there was at least some sense of security. Aarne waited anxiously. His knee bounced up and down as he fiddled with the edge of his jacket sleeve.

"It'll be over soon," Kalevi said, looking less sure of himself than his voice suggested.

The assault continued. Everyone sat stone-faced. In the distance Aarne could hear the explosions and the wails of planes whirring overhead. Air raid signals blared.

After the last plane dropped its bombs and flew away, the captain started the ferry again and travelled down the now quiet canal to the original destination close to the town center. The sailors disembarked, surveying the shelled out buildings, bricks strewn across streets, people covered in dust and soot. The damage was extensive. Buildings were in ruin, and streets were unrecognizable.

"Doesn't even look like the same place," Aarne said. Dust filled the air, threatening to choke them.

"Let's go. Maybe we can get a drink somewhere," Kalevi suggested.

They picked their way over the debris, looking for a restaurant or tavern that might still be open, but noticed two Hitler Youth striding in their direction. The sailors stepped off the sidewalk to let the young men pass but avoided any eye contact.

"Move aside, you dirty eastern workers," one of them said, sneering at the sailors. The other boy spat in Aarne's direction.

"Keep walking," Aarne muttered under his breath. He looked down at the ground, hoping the Germans would lose interest.

The young men kept going, their heavy footsteps moving away into the distance. It wasn't the first time Aarne and his friends had encountered the Nazis during their leaves. He refrained from retaliating when they hurled insults his way, knowing that if either party stopped or retorted, there would surely be a fight. Aarne knew they would not fail to beat or even kill him on the spot with no questions asked. Until now his worries had not been realized. He preferred to stay out of their way.

CHAPTER 5
Danzig, September 1944

—ᴟ—

"*Aufstehen!* Get up!" Clipped German voices reverberated through the stark halls.

Without warning the sailors awoke to the sounds of boots thundering against bare floors, as men in grey-green uniforms infiltrated the interior corridors of the ship.

It was before dawn on September 25, 1944. Fewer than two weeks earlier, the S/S *Wappu* had left Helsinki laden with lumber and wood materials for Poland and Germany. A week later, on September 19, Finland's war with Russia was finally over with the signing of the Moscow Armistice. As part of the treaty, Finland was required to dissolve its connections with the Third Reich. Unaware of these recent developments, the *Wappu* docked in Danzig, Poland—German territory.

As the sounds of Nazi soldiers filled the halls, Aarne scrambled from his narrow bunk, vying for standing room with his three crewmates in the narrow space between the bunks. The air in the room was oppressive. Voices echoed down the hall in waves towards Aarne's cabin.

His breath was shallow as he fumbled for clothes from his trunk. He hustled to pull on a shirt and trousers as the footsteps came closer. With trembling hands he tied the long laces of his leather shoes, trying to keep his balance as his crewmates struggled to dress nearby.

"Passports. Take out your passports," a soldier's voice commanded in the next room.

They were getting closer. Aarne rummaged in his scant belongings to produce his papers. The three sailors, dressed and ready, looked at one another without speaking, their documents shaking in their hands.

Aarne heard the heavy doors as one after the next the Nazis flung them open, each time the footsteps getting closer. As he stood at attention beside his bunk clutching his documents, he searched the faces of his crewmates. They exchanged nervous looks.

In the past the *Wappu*'s connection to the Germans was courteous as the Finns docked in their ports or the Germans guided them past marine mines and into harbours. They were accustomed to the German antiaircraft gunners who were aboard in the event of an airstrike. They were even used to customs officers searching for black-market goods and lining them up for roll call to ensure they were not smuggling people aboard. Sometimes there was trouble in port with the Hitler Youth. But nothing like this had ever happened before.

He waited. He glanced at his cabin mates. Sweat dripped from their hairlines despite the cool air in the cabin.

"Passports." A tall Nazi in a grey uniform stood before them, his huge frame filling the doorway. "Take out your papers."

One by one the soldier confiscated the sailors' documents. Aarne offered his, trying to keep from shaking, barely able to release it into the soldier's outstretched hand. The German briefly studied the small headshot and then eyed the fair-haired, blue-eyed young sailor, gauging his tall, slender frame against the paper's handwritten description.

"Fine," he said, nodding his head curtly, but his voice revealed no emotion. Satisfied, he left the cabin, moving down the hall to the next.

Aarne slumped back into his bunk, listening intently to the happenings down the hall. By the end of the morning, the Nazi soldiers had seized the passports of all sixteen crew members and four female staff members of the *Wappu.*

For the next few days, the Nazis confined the sailors to their tight quarters. Armed guards paced back and forth on deck. The air was heavy and stale. The men became restless. The usual familiarity of their quarters transformed into a prison as the sailors' movements aboard the ship were restricted.

The scent of seawater and salty air mixed with fishy remains from the harbour blew in through the small port windows, providing some relief. The brisk September air reminded the sailors that summer had long since passed.

"How long do you figure they'll keep us in this harbour?" Aarne asked Kalevi. It had been several days since the Nazis had detained the ship.

"Don't know. I suppose they can keep us as long as they want," Kalevi said. "If we could only listen to the radio, we could get some idea about what's going on out there." He kept his voice low, not wanting to draw the attention of the others.

"You have to wonder why they took the radios. What don't they want us to know?" Aarne wondered aloud. "Do people at home even know where we are?"

"They may believe we are in Poland, but that's it, I guess. We should have left this port by now. If the captain couldn't get through before the radios were taken, I'm guessing they'll think we went down at sea."

The two boys paused. It had been a long time since they'd had contact with their homes, but the thought of their families not knowing where they were was almost worse than the thought of the vessel sinking.

"Let's hope they find out what's happening," Aarne said, thinking of the faces of his mother and father in Oulu.

As the days passed, rumours abounded. After the immediate chaos of the first day, the crew settled into an uncomfortable semisilence. The seamen whispered to each other, commiserating and arguing. Their small spaces seemed even tighter, more oppressive now that they were so close to shore but were not permitted to step foot there.

A few days after the detention began, the German soldiers returned.

"Move along! Everyone get out." The sounds of the Nazi soldiers echoed through the bowels of the boat.

Once again Aarne pulled on his khaki trousers and tucked in his shirt with trembling hands. He grabbed a light jacket and quickly tied his best Sunday shoes. At the last minute, before leaving his cabin, he remembered the picture pinned by his bed. He reached up to his bunk, seized the crumpled photograph of the girl from his hometown, and stuffed it into his jacket pocket.

"What's happening?" he mumbled as he fell into step beside one of the crew members.

"Don't know, Aarne. Better be quiet," the sailor replied. "Do what they say."

Aarne glanced at the older man. His face was like stone.

Outside, the crew lined up along the deck. An officer in a crisp uniform stood before them. He walked up and down the line, as if inspecting his troops. He paused and turned to face the sailors, clearing his throat before beginning.

"Don't worry," the German officer said.

Aarne tried to glance at the others from the corners of his eyes.

"Once you are off the ship, we will make arrangements to have you transported to Sweden, and from there you will return to your beloved Finland." The man leaned back on his heels, a slight smile forming at the corner of his mouth. "No need to be concerned."

Aarne looked at the officer's shiny, black jackboots. Would the Germans really send the sailors back? Why couldn't they take the *Wappu*? Were the Germans confiscating it as well?

Aarne had his doubts. By the looks of the others, none of them believed they were going home either.

The Nazi soldiers transported the crew to a large warehouse, carrying whatever personal effects they had managed to gather from their sea trunks. As Aarne entered the nondescript building, the smell of musty air hit his nostrils. The building was almost completely empty. The tall ceiling towered above them. A few small windows let in streams of light, exposing the grimy interior and the dusty concrete floors. There was nowhere to sleep save the bare floor and no facilities. He wondered how long they would have to wait here or if it was just a stopping point on the way to their real destination.

The crew gathered in the corner of the warehouse, soon joined by others.

"Where are you coming from?" Captain Jansen asked as each group entered the expansive space.

The newcomers were from other Finnish ships, the *Mercator* and the *Bore VI*, a total of sixty-one men and ten women, and all had similar stories. Before long, the crew of the *Ellen* would also be arrested. The

Germans had also detained the others sometime after September 19 in the port of Danzig and promised them safe passage to Sweden.

—m—

Days passed.

The sailors received scant daily rations of food and water, barely enough to sustain themselves. Aarne fought hunger and fatigue as he huddled in his section of the warehouse, trying to find space to spread out and sleep.

The sailors compared stories of the Germans' holding them against their will before marching them to the warehouse. One of the sailors from the *Mercator* related a story to Aarne and some others about an incident aboard their boat.

"A few days after being detained," he said, "a fight started between one of the younger sailors and one of the veterans. The older man loved to sing. We used to listen to him at night sometimes. He had a great voice. The two started to argue, but I couldn't catch what it was all about. Maybe it was nothing. Anyway one struck the other, and the real fight started."

A few of the crew of the *Wappu* nodded. They had seen that before. Aarne remembered the frayed nerves they had felt when the Germans had detained them in Danzig.

"Two of our men tried to break up the fight. Somehow the older man—you know, the singer—fell and hit his head against a steel beam. His body crumpled to the ground. He just went limp. I thought he was dead."

The sailor paused, shaking his head slowly. "I didn't think he was going to make it. The blood just pooled under his head and spread across the floorboards. A few of us picked him up and put him on a table. We tried to wrap a shirt around the wound to stop the bleeding. After a few minutes, one of those German soldiers came around and saw him lying in his own blood. The soldier said to us, 'If he is going to die, I'll take care of him,' and then he pointed at his holstered pistol. We couldn't believe it."

Aarne shuddered. He looked around the warehouse at all of the Finnish sailors. What were they doing there?

—∞—

Within a week the Finns moved again. The soldiers pointed their weapons and ordered them to get in lines. Aarne marched through the town over the cobblestone streets, relieved at least to feel the sun on his face, the fresh air in his lungs. *Perhaps we are getting transported to Sweden after all*, he thought. Briefly he let his hopes soar.

When they finally arrived, the soldiers ushered them through a set of double doors into a large, rectangular room. Aarne noticed the wooden floors for dancing, tables gathered around the sides for dinners, and a stage for a band or theatre productions. Before the war, laughter and music would have filled this place. Men smartly dressed in their dark suits and ties would have held beautiful women in their arms, swinging them around the dance floor to a waltz or polka as their skirts swished past one another. The smells of cigarette smoke, liquor, and perfume would have intermingled in the hazy room. Actors and actresses would have paraded across the stage; musicians would have filled the space with music. Now armed guards stood around the hall, dressed in their tidy uniforms, weapons readily accessible.

Aarne followed the men and women into the space as they found whatever tables or pieces of floor they could to rest their bodies. They spoke in hushed tones. Their crumpled clothes told the story of several sleepless nights, and the sharp scent of body odour hung in the air. Aarne's hopes plummeted yet again.

The dance hall was only slightly better than the warehouse. It was smaller and cleaner but still stark and cold.

"There has to be some way out of here," Kalevi said. The two sat on the floor, knees propped up.

"Keep an eye out," Aarne replied. He scanned the room. "Maybe we can get through that opening over there." He gestured discreetly to a small window near the roofline.

That night Aarne, Kalevi, and another young sailor, determined to find a way out, tiptoed past the other slumbering sailors. Several were snoring, and some turned restlessly. Bodies lay across the floor, illuminated only by slim shafts of light falling from the few narrow openings.

"Help me up," Kalevi whispered as he stood on a table. He reached for the window and managed to unlatch it and pop it open. "I think I can make it."

Aarne watched him pull himself through and then climbed up behind him. From the outside he reached down to give his friend a hand up.

Once outside Aarne closed the window, trying not to make a sound. The three crouched along the low-pitched roof, breathing in the night air. It was a refreshing change from the stench hovering in the hall. Aarne watched his breath snake and dissipate into the dark.

At the back of the building, they found a drainpipe. Aarne went first. He lowered himself down, looking both ways for signs of movement. He stood watch as the other two climbed down to the ground.

Sneaking between the buildings and clinging to the shadows, Aarne and his mates crouched low as they moved away from the building. By the time they reached the town centre, they relaxed, sauntering through the stone-paved streets as though they belonged. Between them they had a few German marks in their pockets, which they spent on food and drinks at a local establishment. No one looked at them twice.

For the next two nights, the three helped one another climb through the small window to freedom, always managing to return before first light. After the third escape, one of the older men cornered the three escapees.

"Listen. If you get caught, they will kill you," he said in hushed tones. "You do not want to mess with these men."

"We're not hurting anyone. And we always come back," Aarne said. "We're just having a little fun."

"It needs to stop. Even if you aren't caught out there, someone will find out about it here."

The three boys crossed their arms but hung their heads. Their hope of liberty vanished into the frosty September air. Their nightly escapes ended. As Aarne lay on the bare floor, he looked up at the light shining through the window. *If I went through that window again, I would never return*, he thought. *But*, he asked himself, *where could I possibly go?*

—⁓—

A week passed in the makeshift prison. One morning the click-clacking sound of hobnailed jackboots crossing the wooden floor startled the sailors as they slumped against the dance hall walls. The Nazi officers in their pressed, grey-green uniforms, stamped aluminum insignia displayed on their chests, slate grey trousers tucked into their tall black boots, peaked caps placed securely under their arms, strode towards the long tables set up end to end at the far side of the room. The snap, snap, snap of the latches as they opened their leather attaché cases echoed in the silence. In the back corner, where he sat with his knees tucked to his chest, Aarne began to tremble.

The Finnish sailors were weary, hungry, and dishevelled; the Germans had been confining them for several weeks. They had only enough energy to watch the officers as they took their seats, spreading their documents across a long table. They sat with straight backs in wooden chairs, facing the prisoners.

"Line up over here." A tall, thin man pointed to an area in front of the tables.

The sailors stood in straight rows while the officers eyed the bedraggled men up and down. They showed no expressions on their pale faces.

The men shuffled back and forth on their feet. A single set of jackboots crossed the floor.

"Welcome to Germany." His deep announcer's voice echoed against the walls. "You will have a good life here." Aarne watched his face smile encouragingly at the sailors. "All you need to do is come here and sign up with one of these officers." He walked up and down the rows, looking at the sailors. "You may wish to join the army. Perhaps you would prefer the navy, since you are sailors. Or you may want to join the air force. Maybe you would like to work at a good German factory. Step forward. Sign up."

The sailors glanced nervously at each other, but nobody moved.

"Please, please. You will like Germany. You will be treated well and have much to eat. Life is good in Germany. Sign here with these officers." His easy manner began to show signs of irritation.

"Nobody goes. Nobody signs anything," Captain Jansen instructed the sailors.

One by one the Finnish crews left the row and moved towards the back of the hall in protest. Aarne left the line, turning his back on the officers at the table, and joined a small group of his friends sitting on the floor. The officers remained at the front on their own, smiles changing to scowls; within minutes an ocean-wide expanse had appeared across the dance hall between the Germans and the Finns.

The officers leaned over the table, mumbling to one another. A few minutes later, a member of the Gestapo arrived. His voice thundered through the hall. Angry orders replaced the encouraging words.

"Whoever doesn't work during this war doesn't eat. You must get up. You must sign these papers." For several minutes, the man roared at the sailors.

They listened in fear, but refused to move.

Finally the officers gathered their documents and placed them in their briefcases. The chairs scraped the wooden floor as the men pushed them away from the table. With some relief the sailors listened as the tapping sound of the jackboots diminished in the distance.

But Aarne worried about their fate as he huddled with the others. Transportation to Sweden was a ruse. Finland, his home, seemed very far away.

—⁓—

At dawn on October 21, almost a month after their initial arrest, the sailors, some snoozing in awkward positions on the floor, others dozing in semiseated positions against the walls, awoke as a group of armed Nazi soldiers barged into the hall.

"Time to get moving, you lazy pigs," a soldier shouted, kicking sleeping bodies.

In a matter of minutes, the Finns were standing at attention. Aarne grabbed his jacket before the soldiers drove him outside.

The Germans jostled the sailors down the middle of the street, past shattered buildings and piles of debris. They had no idea where they were headed. Already a few citizens with horses and buggies were beginning their day. Women carrying bundles, trailed by children, stopped to stare as the group passed. The sailors marched to the railroad station, where small, windowless, wooden rail cars stood with open doors on a narrow-gauge railway. The train looked like it was for hauling cattle or wheat, not human beings.

"Get in!" Using the butts of their rifles, the soldiers hit several of the sailors, driving them towards the reddish-brown rail cars.

Aarne's whole body tensed as he witnessed the violence. He tried to stay with his own group, away from the beatings. He pulled himself up and squeezed himself into the car, which was already stuffed full of bodies crushed one against another.

The door of the train shut with a resounding crash, followed by the scraping of the heavy latch into its socket. The guards locked the sailors into the suffocating prison. All that remained was darkness.

CHAPTER 6

Train to Stutthof, October 1944

—ᴟ—

AARNE WAS CRUSHED AGAINST his crewmates. The sailors stood together, shoulder to shoulder, in the cramped railcar as it began to crawl east down the tracks, from the station in Danzig on the Baltic coast to its unknown destination. After living in the dance hall for several weeks with little nourishment and terrible sleeping conditions, Aarne felt overwhelmed by hunger and exhaustion. His body ached, and he felt dizzy, but there was nowhere to sit on the crowded floorboards of the compartment.

The stink of manure and rotted hay filled his nostrils, but he couldn't even raise his hand to wipe his nose. As the train progressed, Aarne's eyes adjusted to the dim light. A faint gleam pierced through the cracks of the wooden walls.

Aarne surveyed the railcar. He regarded his fellow crew members, awed by their strength and determination despite their fear. A few more small holes in the wood and gaps between boards let in glimpses of light and drafts of fresh air. Aarne turned his face towards the remnants of sun, closing his eyes. He became restless: an animal trapped in a cage with no means of escape.

"Where do you think we're going?" Kalevi whispered. He stood beside Aarne, motionless except for his eyes.

"Not home, that's for sure," Aarne replied. "If they were sending us to Finland, they wouldn't have put us on this train."

"What's out there? Can you see anything?" Kalevi motioned with his chin to a narrow chink in the timber. Aarne tried to peer through the slats at the changing landscape.

"Lots of farmland," he said. "We're away from the city."

"Can you see any buildings?" Kalevi asked. "Maybe you can see the name of the stations?"

"Barns and a few houses," Aarne replied, "but I can't see any signs. Mostly just farmers' fields."

The train edged along. The sour air thickened. The men struggled for breath and shuffled from foot to foot. Once in a while, there was a brief exchange, but mostly there was silence. Aarne could hear someone coughing uncontrollably in the corner.

The hours passed. The train stopped several times, but no one came to the door to let them out or air in.

"Lots of forest here," Aarne said to Kalevi over the steady chug of the engines. "Doesn't seem like we are anywhere near the sea. We must be going farther inland."

"Farther from home." Kalevi tried to stand on his tiptoes to see past the shoulders of his shipmates. "Can't see a thing from here."

With an abrupt jolt, the train stopped again. Aarne tried to see through the slats.

"Just trees," he said as he caught the sharp scent of pine drifting into the compartment.

Aarne wondered if they would finally be free of this narrow prison or if it was yet another stop en route to their journey's end.

A few minutes passed. The sounds of boots hitting the gravel. German voices calling out orders.

The latch released with a grind, and the heavy wooden door grumbled as it slid open. A rush of wind flooded the stifling space, and even the weakest opened their eyes and their mouths to inhale the fresh air. Light flooded through the open doorway, revealing a bedraggled group of exhausted and hungry sailors. On the other side, guards in crisp uniforms greeted them with scowls.

"Get out. Faster." The SS guard bellowed his orders.

One by one the Finns stepped down from the railcar. A guard struck the nearest man, who stumbled and fell to his hands and knees. The guard gave him a swift kick.

"Get up." He scowled as though the man was to blame.

Angry dogs barked and paced, baring their teeth. Blows and curses continued as the others disembarked from their respective railcars and joined the growing throng.

Aarne blinked against the sun. With stiff limbs, he stepped to the platform, nearly tripping from the height of the boxcar. Scanning the landscape for the first time through squinted eyes, he gradually adjusted to the harsh daylight, looking for some indication of his location.

The train had stopped at a small station, positioned at the crossing of a long main street stretching far into the flat distance and a narrower side road leading into the forest. Across the tree-lined street, Aarne could see waves of farmland extending to the horizon. Tall pines towered over the newly arrived sailors. Golden brown and red leaves crunched under their shoes as they walked along the uneven cobblestones. The chill in the air reminded Aarne that fall had arrived and winter was coming.

"Get moving." The Nazi guards used the butts of their rifles to push them forward.

As though woken from a dream, Aarne and Kalevi followed the guards' directions. The tight feeling in Aarne's stomach that had plagued him throughout the train ride intensified. He tried to avoid the steely glare of the Germans and the sharp fangs of their dogs.

Through the soaring trees behind the train stop, a pretty, white villa with a lovely front garden sat on a hill, surrounded by a picket fence. Looking briefly from the stone path, Aarne wondered who lived there. Later other prisoners would tell him the villa belonged to the commandant, SS-Sturmbannführer Paul Werner Hoppe, and his family. The scene was oddly picturesque.

Aarne and Kalevi glanced at one another but dared not speak.

The Germans drove the Finnish crews down the side road, past the commandant's villa, armed guards threatening to hit or shoot them as they marched. To the right a pack of German shepherds barked and sprang at them from behind the wooden gate as they passed a red brick doghouse. To their left stately pines lined the cobblestone street. Aarne could see only the darkness of a deep forest through the dense foliage. The sailors continued marching down the road, the brick and wood fence continuing for several metres, as the guards steadily hurled abuse and used their rifles like cattle prods.

Aarne's mind raced. He glanced at the faces of the others, but they were expressionless. Only Kalevi's face mirrored his own: pale skin, clenched jaw, and saucer eyes.

The SS guards swung open the first gate. The Finnish men and women reluctantly flooded through it. Beyond the entrance, the view of a long, two-storey building constructed of red brick startled Aarne. A series of white windows with six panes each spanned across the second-floor balcony. On the first level, a glassed-in foyer led to double doors facing a circular moat. At its centre a large, peaked structure dominated the landscape. It was both impressive and formidable.

"Is that where we're going?" Aarne turned to Kalevi. It didn't make any sense.

"I doubt it," Kalevi replied. "That's probably where the guards stay. They're not likely to let us in there."

Aarne agreed. The immense structure reminded him of another building burned in his memory. On summer afternoons in Oulu, he and his friends, Matti and Kauko, had quietly approached an abandoned factory, a four-storey red brick building with ten-by-ten windows gleaming in the midday sun. Weighed down by the handfuls of stones stuffed into their pant pockets, the boys clawed their way up the trees, each carrying a homemade slingshot. From their precarious perches on the branches, the boys took aim, counting the shots that shattered the glass, hooting with delight at every direct hit. One by one the boys broke almost every window in that factory. The memory made Aarne frown. He longed to be back at home with his friends, safe in his hometown, instead of waiting endlessly for the end to begin.

The guards steered the group past the less striking brick SS-guardhouse and Political Department barracks on the left, all the time barraging them with commands and swinging their batons and rifle barrels.

"Wait here." A guard motioned for the group to halt.

They stopped before the Political Department, supervised by a Gestapo officer who received the information about the incoming. From there, transport lists were organized, camp numbers assigned, interrogations conducted, and prisoners' fates determined. It would take some time to process the Finnish sailors and decide where they would be lodged in the camp.

For now Aarne waited. The sailors stayed, their guards ignoring them utterly. A dark wood gate barred further movement. Aarne later learned the prisoners had named it the death gate. He examined it with the dreadful feeling that it was the only thing left between him and hell.

The gate was constructed in a diamond pattern of wooden slats. A set of stairs angled up from a low building on the left to the imposing watchtower positioned over the gates. Aarne shivered when he noticed the armed guards glaring from above.

Hours passed. The guards continued to disregard their presence.

"Is this a labour camp?" Aarne finally asked. "I don't see any labourers."

"Maybe they're working elsewhere," Kalevi said. "Those must be the barracks." He indicated several buildings on the other side of the gate.

Aarne faced the flat vista, three rows of one-storey wooden huts to the right and left of two wide, straight roads. A double electrified barbed-wire fence surrounded the area. SS stood guard in watchtowers at each corner and at intervals along the fence around the camp. At this time of day, it seemed eerily quiet. Aarne could see a towering brick structure at the eastern end of the site, smoke wafting from its eighteen-metre-tall chimney. The putrid smell of burning and the trail of dark smoke dissolving into the sky would become constant reminders of the brevity of life.

As Aarne and the other sailors clustered together outside the gates, few spoke and then only in covert whispers. No one wanted the attention of the guards, who, for the time being, occupied themselves with other matters.

"Look there." Aarne motioned to Kalevi. "That man hasn't moved in ages."

Aarne pointed to the figure of a lone male prisoner standing in an open area. His pale, gaunt face hung slack from his bones. His striped hat partially covered a head of stubbly hair. His shoulders drooped heavily under the weight of a blue and white striped coat; the tips of his fingers were barely visible under the oversized sleeves. His legs threatened to give out at any moment, yet he stood motionless, as he had done for many hours.

"Why do you suppose he's there?" Aarne asked, unsure if it was the cooling late afternoon air or the sight of the solitary figure that made him shudder.

"He's probably being punished for something," Kalevi replied. They both stared at the fellow, who looked more like a fragile sculpture than a living human being.

For several hours no one came to speak to the strangers as they waited outside the death gate. Aarne's stomach grumbled, and his mouth felt dry and swollen. He scanned the faces of his older shipmates. Most stood stoically, as though waiting in line at the grocer's with their food stamps. If they were afraid, they weren't showing it. *If there is such a thing as sisu—the indefinable combination of determination, bravery, and strength in the face of adversity that Finns admire—these sailors possess it*, thought Aarne. He took a deep breath and tried to steady the nerves flaring in his belly.

Anxious and afraid, he was faced with new concerns. The sky transformed from a cloudless blue to pinks and purples laced with gold as the sun began to lower on the horizon behind the forest of pine trees. He pulled his light jacket close around his body, stamping his feet to keep warm. Steam escaped from his lips with every breath, travelling upward like the sour smoke from the distant chimney.

"Look over there, Aarne," Kalevi said. They both turned to the sounds of footsteps shuffling in the distance along the cobblestones.

Arriving in columns of five and carrying a variety of farm tools, a contingent of bone-thin and exhausted prisoners trooped down the path and through the gaping gate. The members of the work group were barely able to place one foot before the other. Their work tools looked like heavy weights in their hands.

Aarne turned to Kalevi. "If they are the ones doing hard labour, you would think they would be some of the strongest people in this place. They don't look too good to me," he whispered.

"I don't think they've seen a scrap of food in months," Kalevi said. "If they are the workers, what do the others look like?"

Aarne looked at Kalevi's astonished expression, trying to hide the fear that was clawing up his body. Every instinct told him to flee, but there was nowhere to go.

All eyes widened as the Finns became engrossed in the details of the prisoners trailing past. Their pungent body odour flooded the air and persisted long after they passed. Their wooden shoes drudged up dust as they dragged their feet against the road. Their thick camp clothes, threadbare with tatters, were covered in dirt and grime. The prisoners avoided eye contact with the newly arrived, looking vaguely in the distance or at the ground in front, eyes vacant. Their shoulders hunched so low, their arms seemed to drag along the ground.

Once in a while, a guard cursed and shouted at someone to hurry up, his voice matching the bark of his angry dog. Aarne watched as a guard delivered a random blow to a straggler at the back of the column. The prisoner stumbled over his own feet before rushing to rejoin the group.

As the work group entered the bowels of the camp, the Finnish sailors stood at the death gate in stunned silence. Aarne stared in horror. *Beyond the gate*, he wondered, *what hell awaited?*

CHAPTER 7
Death Gate, October 1944

—∿—

STANDING BEFORE THE GATE for hours, with a view of the pine forests, the watchtowers, and the electrified barbed-wire fence, Aarne contemplated his fate. How could he survive in this place? What would become of him and his crew mates? Would he ever see his family again?

Shortly after the columns of emaciated bodies filed through the death gate, the Finnish sailors observing them in silence, the guards finally appeared.

"Get moving!" one demanded. Aarne stood at attention, watching the guard's every move.

The sailors filed through the wide gate, into the bowels of the camp, past several banks of barracks. A guard ordered them to halt. Another guard went inside and, after a few minutes, came back, shaking his head. He spoke in a hushed tone to the other guards and then turned to the prisoners.

"Men go this way," he said, pointing east. "Women, you go that way."

Aarne would later learn that the few females from the ships, including the *Wappu*'s head cook, kitchen hand, housekeeper, and cleaner, were housed in blocks I and VIII of the so-called old camp with other female prisoners. The men would be housed elsewhere.

"What's happening?" Aarne asked. "Where are they taking us now?"

"I have no idea," Kalevi whispered. "Just don't draw any attention to yourself."

Aarne and the crew members of the *Wappu*, the *Bore VI*, and the *Mercator* kept marching. The sun was low on the horizon, casting long shadows over the fallen leaves as the Finns walked and walked. After about two kilometres, they finally arrived at another camp enclosure, with several structures like those of the main camp.

Four large barracks stood in the field. Aarne's group was led to block III. As the sailors streamed in, Norwegians met them—inhabitants of Sonderlager, or the special camp.

As soon as the Norwegians realized the new arrivals were Finns, they were filled with questions. They wanted to know everything they could about the outside world, the war, their home country, and the Finns. It didn't take long before they found a common language. A few of the sailors spoke Norwegian and explained their circumstances. In turn the Finns wanted to know about the Norwegians.

"We're all policemen, imprisoned in Stutthof since before Christmas last year," one said. "There are two hundred and seventy-one of us."

"How can that be? Why were you arrested in the first place?" the captain asked.

The Finns were stunned. How could anyone survive this place for almost a year? Aarne couldn't help but wonder if the same fate awaited him. How long would the Germans hold them?

The Norwegian looked at Captain Jansen and sighed. "Our government told us we had to sign a document of loyalty to the Third Reich. But we refused. The government sent us here.

"At first it wasn't so bad," the man continued. "We had it much better than the prisoners in the main camp. The guards treated us fairly well. We had enough to eat. But they kept trying to get us to cooperate. They wanted us to proclaim our allegiance and work for the Nazis. We kept declining." The man shook his head. "Now it's not too good. We have less food, the work is hard, and they treat us poorly. I guess they've given up on us signing away our souls."

Aarne entered his block, relieved, at least, to remain with his shipmates. He looked around the stark wooden hut. Each barrack was approximately sixty metres long and twelve and a half metres wide. In the middle of the block were the toilets and washing facilities. Several round, concrete basins for washing, looking like oversized flowerpots, were scattered throughout the space, but there was no soap or disinfectant.

Aarne entered his sleeping room behind several shipmates. Rows of three-tiered bunks lined the walls, each the length of a man's arm spread but much narrower in width, with only a little space between each. The top bunk reached nearly to the low-pitched roof, with scant space between the tiers. The lowest sat close to the wooden-planked floor.

Although it was a crisp evening, the windows were wide open. Aarne shivered, feeling the dampness seep through his clothes. Even once the windows were latched, the walls and roof were so thin he thought he could feel a breeze as he stood in the centre of the room.

The fatigued men collapsed, anxious for some rest after enduring the long day's events. Aarne hunched at the edge of his bed on a lower bunk, surveying the sparse room. Apart from the beds, a small, unlit heater at the end of the room was the only furniture.

"Try to get some sleep, Aarne," a sailor in the bunk above said. "No doubt they'll have us up with first light."

"I'll try," he replied.

He reached into his jacket pocket and pulled out his creased photograph. For a long time, he stared at the picture of the pretty, young girl from Oulu, remembering how he had found the photograph in the snow. For months now he had carried the girl's picture on sea voyages, a reminder of home and a beautiful young girl he had once met. Now he wedged it between the wall and his bunk, careful to hide it from plain view.

"Is that your girlfriend, Aarne?" The sailor in the next bunk grinned. Apart from Kalevi, who was four months younger, Aarne was the youngest and was used to the older crew's frequent needling.

"Yes, she's my girl. She's back home in Oulu," he said. He gave the man a look that made him pause. Aarne hoped he wouldn't ask her name.

"Pretty girl," the man said. He turned in his narrow bunk and left Aarne alone. The other sailors had left behind girlfriends or wives, families of their own. One of the sailors was a newlywed, having married just before the last crossing began. Everyone was missing someone.

Maybe after the war I will find this girl, Aarne thought. He stared at the snapshot for a long time. It reminded him of another engrained in his memory.

Aarne pictured the grainy photograph of his parents he had so often passed by at home. It had probably been taken during their engagement in 1916. Twenty-two-year-old Anna Liisa Pohjola looked at the camera with slightly upturned lips. She wore a dark, collared blouse with tiny buttons, tucked into a long, dark skirt. She had a pretty face with heavy eyelids over her deep-set eyes. Her fiancé, Jussi Kovala, just turned twenty, gazed off to the left of the camera, his double-breasted suit looking somewhat too large for his lean frame, his hair neatly trimmed. He looked rather serious.

Anna Liisa, a petite woman, wore her long, thick, chestnut hair in a braided knot bundled at her neck. While dating, Jussi had once teased her about her thick bun—a story she often repeated to her family over the years.

"You must have a ball of wool hidden in your hair," Jussi had said. "Otherwise how could that bun be so full?"

"I'll show you if I have a ball of yarn in there." Slowly, Anna Liisa had released the pins from the bun at the nape of her neck, letting her thick, beautiful hair fall down around her shoulders.

It must have sealed the deal: the two were married in a simple wedding on June 1, 1916. After their wedding lunch at Linnansaari, Jussi carved their initials into the woodwork.

Memories of his mother and father reminded Aarne of their worried looks as they had said good-bye on the day he had left home. Did they know their youngest son was in Stutthof? Did they wonder when he would return home? He recalled his brothers and sister and the girl in the photograph. Tears formed in his eyes and silently slipped down his cheeks. Maybe the girl was his guardian angel, for he had already survived the many dangers aboard the merchant marine ship as it travelled from one dangerous port to another; perhaps she could somehow help him now to survive this terrible ordeal.

Aarne rested his head on the thin mattress of wood shavings and dirty straw, hoping to close his eyes for a few hours and awake from this nightmare. The October night was bitterly cold. Aarne pulled the old, cotton blanket under his chin, but it provided little protection from the numbing air whistling in through the cracks.

As he stared at the bunk above him, he heard the sounds of his prison mates, the beds groaning as the sleepy shifted in the small space, a few scattered snores signalling that some were able to sleep. A stifled sob from a corner broke the silence. A few muffled moans escaped the lips of the restless.

A soft shaft of light from the stark windows cast the shadow of a cross from the window casings on the hut's wooden floor. Aarne imagined he could hear the sounds of water crashing against the shore in the far distance, and sometimes he thought he caught the faint whiff of the sea as the wind blew through the cracks in the walls. He stared at the shadow on the floorboards until he drifted in and out of a fitful sleep.

In a dream he is standing by the sea near his home on Nummikatu, in his old Kuusiluoto neighbourhood. He is not yet ten years old. The sea is calm as the sun sets slowly on the horizon, creating a cascade of colours in the sky and water. The tall, white birch trees stand stately beside the coast while waves gently play against the shore, as they have for centuries. It is after supper, and his mother and father sit with the neighbours around the picnic tables, laughing and gossiping over coffee while the children play by the water's edge, skipping smooth, round rocks over the shiny surface. Circular patterns dot the seashore where the rocks briefly touch the water.

Suddenly he is at sea, on a little boat that is, for him, a warrior ship. He has the only boat in the neighbourhood with a motor, one his father has fashioned for him; behind him he tugs five or six of his friends' vessels. The sea gently rolls as the sunlight bounces off the small, white peaks of the waves. Only the brilliance of the water defies the blue of the sky.

Now he is near Hietasaari, a favourite island in the harbour. His navy of friends is challenging the Hietasaari boys in the open water. A mini war at sea erupts, with oars clashing and water spraying as the sea's swells toss their little boats. The boys laugh and scream.

Farther south another group forms its own navy, but Aarne's group knows better than to mess with them; their sea tactics are rough and fearsome.

The sky darkens, and the sea begins to toil. His little boat is all alone in the giant swells, tipped and tossed up and down under the low-hanging clouds. He can no longer see the other boats. The shore is a narrow line in the distance, barely visible between sea and sky.

CHAPTER 8

Sonderlager, Autumn 1944

—⚉—

AARNE'S EYES ADJUSTED TO the still-dark room as the sounds of the *kapos*, the prisoners that the SS appointed to keep discipline, bombarded the block. Through the window the sun was a hazy sliver on the horizon. He rose from his bunk and fumbled to tie the worn laces of his scuffed leather shoes. Every day was the same. He was losing track of how many mornings he had awoken before dawn, how many hours he had toiled in the fields, how many nights he had tried to sleep.

"Aufstehen! Get up!" The voices were always demanding, insistent, inhuman.

He splashed his face with the cold water that trickled from the tap, thankful for even that amount since the water was turned on only once every few weeks. By then his loose clothes were encrusted with the grime of the camp and the dust of the fields. The stench in the hut was palpable. He glanced at his barrack mates. They too looked thin and frayed.

"What's for breakfast?" one of the sailors asked.

"Very funny," another replied. "It's always the same, day in and day out."

"Better than no food at all," Aarne said.

"Very true."

Aarne followed the men to the line, eager for his rations. He held out his bowl for the scant meal. It was unceremoniously doled out to each of the men in turn by a scowling prisoner. Aarne didn't dare make eye contact and moved on as quickly as he could.

Outside he sat on the cold ground, his shoulders squeezed between two Finnish shipmates. He picked up the dry, stale bread with his dirty, calloused fingers. A meagre layer of barely visible margarine did nothing for the flavour. It tasted like sawdust and did little to quell the hunger that had settled permanently into his belly.

He sipped the lukewarm, watery coffee. It was bitter but helped the hard particles of bread dissolve and was safer, some said, than drinking the contaminated camp water. At least at some point it was likely to have been boiled. As he took his last bite, licking the crumbs from his fingers, Aarne thought momentarily that saving a bit would have been a good idea. Bread was a precious commodity he could exchange for much needed clothing, paper, or soap. A scrap was more valuable than gold behind the barbed wires, but it was too difficult to refrain from eating it with hunger constantly gnawing at him from the inside out.

The horizon was brightening, from a pale yellow strip to pink to pale blue before bleeding gradually into the darkness of the early morning.

Aarne scraped every last speck from the bottom of his bowl and then ran his container to the next person in line, knowing he too would be eagerly awaiting the awful meal.

In the distance explosions disturbed the early morning. The Russians seemed to be getting closer and closer.

"Roll call," a guard called.

"Let's go, Aarne," Kalevi said.

Aarne followed him to the square, his tired body sore from labour and lack of sleep. He watched as some of the others, the fortunate ones who had traded for, stolen, or somehow acquired eating vessels, attached their tin cups and bowls to their clothes with strings, ready for the next meal. He wondered how he could get one of those valuable containers for himself.

As the prisoners moved into formation, the area they left behind was spotless; not a morsel was wasted. Aarne's stomach began to rumble again as he waited for the guards to begin. The prisoners stood in long rows as the SS men and the trusties carefully surveyed them. He tried to steal glances at the other prisoners, but he feared drawing the attention of the guards. Better to remain lifeless.

The guards counted each row. In the line ahead, Aarne could see his captain, standing motionless. To his right Kalevi stood at attention. He looked more hunched these days, but he still managed a weak smile in his direction. Nearby the ship's machinist shuffled his feet. Aarne glimpsed a guard striding towards him. He tried to straighten up, to look strong. In fact he felt like his knees might collapse. The guard passed by, yelling at a man behind him. He heard a whack followed by a whimper. He couldn't turn around to see who had received the punishment. He didn't even wonder why. No reason was needed. He was tired. More tired than he had ever felt in his life. And the day was just beginning.

One by one the guards counted and recounted the prisoners. Then they gave curt instructions for the day, and the rows disbanded. The morning's procedure went relatively smoothly. *The guards*, Aarne thought, *want us to get to work as quickly as possible.*

He saw his shipmates hustle from the tidy rows towards their *kommandos*, their assigned labour squads. Many of them, like Marttson, the ship's carpenter, and Mikander, Karlsson, and Hyöti, the machinists, had specific skills, and the Germans had assigned them to the workshops onsite, like the German Equipment Works (DAW) or the local brickyards. The Germans also hired out some of the inmates to private industries and agricultural facilities or employed them onsite at the Focke-Wulff airplane factory.

Aarne joined his work group, grabbing a farming tool from the pile before lining up for the march to the potato fields. For the first few weeks of incarceration, Aarne, Kalevi, and a few of the other young sailors from the Finnish ships had not been assigned specific kommandos but were given a variety of jobs around the camp, like cutting and carrying stumps for firewood. The work was backbreakingly difficult, and they had no rest. The kapo, an inmate assigned as a labour-group supervisor, was a vile-looking man with a permanent grimace. He stood above the prisoners, ready to beat anyone who appeared to be working too slowly.

Aarne kept his head down but his eye on the supervisor, trying to avoid the rage that could flare up at any given moment. The boys barely spoke to one another as they worked, fearing reprisal. Aarne's sheer exhaustion made even brief communication a chore.

Now, as he fell into step, following the group outside the gates to gather the fall harvest, he filled his lungs with the cool morning air. It was demanding labour, but the fine soil was fairly easy for digging, and compared to the stark grey interior of the camp, the wide rolling field was a welcome sight.

"Move on," the guard demanded sternly, but his face was expressionless as the group paraded by, a rifle slung across his back.

Aarne kept his eyes forward. His mind wandered to a group of young boys walking in the tall grass of an open field, a rifle gripped in small hands. It hadn't taken Aarne and Matti much convincing to get Kauko to borrow his father's rifle. Kauko lived across the street from the leather factory. They decided to cross the field towards the old factory buildings. Every once in a while, Aarne surveyed the area, but no one was in sight. They settled for a location not far from their target, an old warehouse, and built a little platform in the ditch using discarded wood and broken branches, the tall grasses providing good coverage for their position.

As he lay prone on the platform, Aarne felt like a real soldier. He eyed the target, one eye squinting. He slowed his breathing and held steady, aiming at a small spot on the dome.

"Anyone there?" Aarne whispered.

"All clear," Matti replied.

Aarne pulled the trigger. Within seconds a pop echoed across the field, and dust rose from the top of the dome.

"A hit," Kauko said with delight.

"Duck. Someone might have heard that," Matti said. The three boys lowered their heads against the wooden platform, each boy grinning from ear to ear.

Kauko raised his head slightly, scanning from left to right.

"All clear. Reload," he said.

Aarne passed the rifle to Matti, who was already in position, elbows on the platform, feet splayed out behind him like a soldier preparing for an ambush. Each boy took his shot in turn, thrilled when they made direct hits and anxious that they might be caught.

Now, as he trooped to and from the fields, he tried to position himself between the other prisoners, where the guards were less likely to notice him or beat him for some infraction with the butt of a rifle. The weapons slung on the guards' shoulders sent shivers down his spine. This was no game. If a beating didn't kill him, it might make him unable to work. If he couldn't work, he would be useless. That was a death sentence.

He briefly remembered the work contingent he had seen entering the death gate when he had first arrived at the camp and wondered if he looked as bedraggled now as they had then. He remembered too a few individuals he had seen while walking through the grounds of the main camp with Kalevi.

"Look at them. Who do you think they are?" he had whispered.

"I heard someone call them *krypels*," Kalevi replied, "because they're so crippled they can barely stand on their own. I don't think that one has much longer on this Earth." Kalevi nodded in the direction of an old man.

"He looks like a walking skeleton," Aarne said. He looked down briefly at his own thinning frame then watched the fellow dragging himself towards the huts, eyes lifelessly searching the bare ground. His face was so gaunt, it looked like his bones were covered in the thinnest layer of taut skin, exposing huge eyes and protruding cheekbones. His clothes hung limply from his shoulders, further exaggerating his tragic stature. Bony fingers protruded from the hands at the ends of his wire-thin arms. Once in a while, the man leaned down to pick some scrap from the ground, fumbling to get the small seed of food into his mouth. The two boys stood as though watching a funeral procession. A sense of sadness and solemnity wrapped its arms around Aarne, embracing him with a cold chill.

Now Aarne took a deep breath of the crisp autumn morning, a welcome relief from the stale air of the barracks, thankful he was not one of the krypels. He felt the warmth of the sun against his face as it rose above the tree line. At the edge of the field, the evergreens provided a dark backdrop for the cornucopia of red and orange leaves. Above, pancake clouds speckled the expansive sky. The sweet scent of new pota-toes mixed with the pungent odour of manure as the men struggled to dig out the earth's bounty.

Aarne struck his shovel into the soil. It was going to be a long day.

"Back to work, you lazy pigs." The guard swung at a prisoner with a long stick, hitting him against his hunched back.

Aarne's shovel dug deeper and swung swiftly. He did not look up.

—◊◊◊—

After several hours of labour, as the sun settled high above the firs and pines, a guard ordered Aarne and his mates to stop working for the mid-day meal. Aarne lined up for his portion of the camp's tasteless, watery soup, hoping for a ladleful of some half-rotten beets, turnips, or perhaps potatoes from the bottom of the pot instead of the water from the top. He watched with disappointment as the soup poured into his bowl from the server. Nothing but liquid again.

Aarne sat on the hard ground, grateful for the brief rest. Too tired to speak, he focused on the bit of slop at the bottom of his bor-rowed bowl. He dipped his grimy fingers into the tepid liquid, licking them to prevent even a drop from satiating the dirty ground below, which soaked in each drop as eagerly as the prisoners downed the soup.

Aarne scrambled to eat his rations, scraping the bottom of the bowl clean. His meal devoured, he scratched the bowl dry. He picked himself off the ground with great effort, his muscles already aching.

"Get back to work, you pigs," the guard said. "Get going. Faster."

Another guard shoved one of the prisoners as he stumbled past.

Aarne picked up his shovel. Dragging it along the ground, he found his place and resumed the endless digging.

—◊◊◊—

One afternoon, as Aarne was digging the marshy soil near the pump house, sweat dripping from his brow, he heard a strange sound.

Tsuuuuut.

Aarne looked up. He saw nothing. He continued to prod the ground for potatoes.

Tsuuuuuuut.

Aarne heard the whistle again.

This time the man at the pump motioned to him. It was difficult to determine what he was trying to say, but Aarne decided he should stay nearby. He had seen this prisoner working the pump to keep the water under control in the fields on many occasions, but they had never spoken before.

What does he want with me? Aarne wondered. He continued to toil, occasionally glancing up with curiosity.

After a few minutes, a heavy thud sounded near his feet. A potato. He looked up at the smiling man, who nodded to him to take the gift. Before Aarne did, he searched the field for the guards. Their attention was elsewhere for the time being. Cautiously he reached down and picked up the piping hot potato.

The spud was scorching in his swollen fingertips. He breathed in its scent. It smelled like his mother's kitchen. His eyes darted across the field as he took a big bite. The pump man grinned at Aarne, his eyes twinkling as he took a mouthful of his own potato.

Aarne's teeth sliced through the soft exterior of the delightful food, its skin brown with dirt and wrinkled from the heat. The centre was hard, only partially cooked, but the outside was warm and satisfying in a way about which the watery soup could only dream. The flavour filled his mouth like an explosion. The heat travelled through his body and into his stomach, where it quickly filled the tiny space for the first time in weeks. It was the best thing he had ever tasted.

Aarne wanted to thank the pump man. When he looked up, however, he was gone. Aarne continued digging.

This time his shovel felt lighter.

—⚉—

The clear sky provided no protection from the beaming sun despite the chilly air. Beneath his thin clothes, Aarne's skin was drenched. As the hours passed, he felt like a machine, repeating each action over and over, trying not to displease the guards but feeling weaker and weaker with each passing minute. His hands were blistered, his back strained, and his head swam. As the sun began to descend, he shivered, the sweat cooling against his skin on a layer of dirt and grime. If only those coatings would provide him with some warmth or protection from the harsh elements. The setting sun provided one relief: work was nearly done.

One evening, after a long day of pulling potatoes from the fields, Aarne joined his kommando for the slog back to camp. His shovel felt heavy in his hands.

"Move faster," the SS man said.

Aarne struggled to keep his feet in step. After twelve hours of heavy labour, his muscles were tense, and his back ached. He could barely see the road ahead. The day was by no means over. Aarne swung his shovel on his back and walked towards the column that was already forming.

He lingered near the end of the line while the group started the procession, and the guards began to hassle and berate them as usual. He noticed another man holding back from the row. He thought he recognized the prisoner but had never spoken to him. Sometimes they even worked side by side. The man didn't speak Finnish or any of the other languages Aarne had learned as a sailor aboard the *Wappu*. Soundlessly, the man gestured to Aarne, and they both looked towards the potato storage area.

Without a word, careful to ensure that the guards did not notice their movements, they snuck towards the shed. The door was unfastened. Aarne pushed it open and cringed as it creaked. The smell of potatoes filled his nostrils, and the sight of them piled high made him salivate. Without hesitating he grabbed one and began devouring it. The other man did the same. Neither spoke.

The potato was hard, and its exterior was covered in a layer of dirt, but Aarne took no notice. It was food. He chewed quickly, taking as many bites as his mouth could handle.

The sound of teeth chomping was interrupted by the thunder of jackboots against the hard ground.

"Halt!" The guard commanded.

Aarne did. The partially eaten potatoes plopped to the ground.

"What do you have there?" The guard grabbed a piece of wood from a stack beside the shed. He held it up as if to beat the stricken prisoners.

The other prisoner acted instantly. He jolted past the guard and ran towards the camp.

Run, Aarne thought.

A second later the guard swung the stick, striking Aarne on the back of the head with enormous force. He fell to the ground. Everything turned black.

Aarne woke with his cheek pressed against the soil. His head hurt. His back stung. His eyes were blurry. He tried to get off the ground, but waves of pain pulsated through his body. It wasn't clear how long he had been out, but when he looked around he could see the SS guard in the distance, pursuing the other prisoner with his makeshift weapon poised above him.

Dazed and afraid, Aarne pulled himself to his feet and hurried towards the camp. He joined the back of a column, hoping no one else would notice or identify him for further punishment. He searched the faces of the prisoners for his fellow potato thief but could not see him in the line. He hoped the man outran the SS guard but could never be sure.

—⁂—

At camp the rest of the kommandos gathered for the evening roll call. Their collective exhaustion made forming the straight lines and waiting to be counted a torment. Aarne hoped the count would be quick, but he knew it could be drawn out for some time. Occasionally a weakened prisoner was found in a hut or in the yard, too fragile to move to roll call. Sometimes the guards found a body of someone who had not survived the gruelling workday. If anyone attempted to escape, SS men and dogs were sent to track him, leaving the camp's prisoners to stand in the square until he was returned. The others would remain standing at attention until the prisoner was accounted for or an escape confirmed.

Aarne tried to keep his legs from crumpling below him. His head pounded from hitting the ground. His body ached, and hunger grew from the pit of his stomach, threatening to devour him whole. As he glanced around, he saw his crewmates standing in the columns, shoulders hunched, faces dragged, and eyes vacant. Their clothes hung on their shrinking frames.

With any luck, the guards would not make them stand in the roll call square for hours on end, as they were known to do, making the inmates perform repetitive exercises regardless of weather for some infraction or other. Perhaps it was for sport.

Even worse, if a whole group offended the guards in some way, they were punished by losing their rations for the day. Aarne shuddered. Fortunately everyone was accounted for, and a meal was in his future.

Supper was more of the same watery soup, eaten with his swollen, cramped fingers. Its vague warmth was a welcome relief, even if it did little to appease his appetite. Death by starvation was common, and Aarne wondered how quickly a healthy man could become the walking dead.

—⁂—

Day after day Aarne slogged in the potato fields. He could hear planes strafing their marks through the forest of pines as the front lines moved towards the camp. Bombs buzzed through the air. Explosions echoed as more planes hit targets in the distance. Aarne feared the sounds of the battle but realized the arrival of the Russians could also mean the liberation of the camp. Sources said the Soviet troops were already nearing East Prussia and Pomerania, moving steadily towards the camp. He had even heard rumours that the Germans had already made plans to evacuate KL Stutthof and its filial camps if the Russians came too close.

Aarne could barely remember a time when the sounds of war did not ring through his head. The Winter War had arrived like a fury in his hometown, although the front lines had been many kilometres away, in the Karelian Isthmus. Aarne closed his eyes, remembering how the incendiaries had come down by the hundreds. That winter the Russians had dropped large drums containing several bombs that spun as they fell, scattering firebombs in all directions. The sight of bombs littering the snowfield was etched in Aarne's mind: they had burned like glowing candlesticks against the pure white snow, saturating the air with an unusually pungent smell he could never forget.

Now, as Aarne struggled to remove the potatoes one by one from the fields near Stutthof, he listened as bombs burst nearby. They filled him with a strange mixture of dread and hope.

—⚉—

"Hey, boys, I have something for you," said one of the Norwegians as he entered their barracks. The wind whipped in through the open door.

"What do you have there?" the captain asked. The men gathered around to see what was hidden in the brown wrapping.

"Just a little bit of smoked salmon. Some chocolate. Maybe some other tasty treats. Anything interesting to you?" He smiled, clearly pleased that he could offer even this small gift.

Aarne leaned in to see what he had. A bond had grown between the Finnish sailors and the Norwegian policemen. Most of the Scandinavians tended to stick together, even when moving around the camp and interacting with the other prisoners.

Aarne's mouth watered. The Norwegian distributed the items from his Red Cross care package. So far the Finns hadn't received anything, but the Norwegians were still getting packages from home periodically. The men passed the dried, salted fish around the block, each taking a small portion.

"Enjoy it all before someone takes it," the Norwegian advised. "You never know when the guards will be hungry."

"Kiitos," Aarne said as he accepted some of the smoked fish. He sat on the edge of his bunk before eating every bit of the tasty treat.

Aarne knew that the Norwegians often shared their Red Cross packages—if they were able to give them away before the guards stole them, that was. Sometimes they hoisted the packages over the fence to the new camp, where most of the Jewish inmates were housed. While everyone suffered in Stutthof, the Jewish prisoners suffered beyond compare. More and more Jewish men and women were arriving every week. It was clear that their conditions were getting even worse than the rest of the camp's with the arrival of each new transport.

Aarne ate his fish in silence, savouring every bite. He listened as the men discussed the rumours that had spread as rapidly as typhus through the camp. The Russians were advancing.

"The Germans won't let the Russians take us alive," said Erik, a tall Norwegian in an Italian army jacket.

Aarne took notice as a small group of sailors gathered.

"A fellow I know from the main camp said they heard it from another prisoner who heard it on the radio when he was working in the command building."

"Sounds like a legitimate source," someone said with a chuckle.

"What does that mean for us?" Aarne asked.

"If the Russians come soon enough, they can liberate the camp before the Germans can do anything about it," Erik said.

"But if they don't, the Nazis will kill us first," another replied.

"I heard they are going to evacuate the camp. March us all out of Poland until we get to Germany," Kalevi said.

"Why would they do that?" Aarne asked. "There are hundreds, even thousands of prisoners here. It doesn't make any sense."

"They got us all here in the first place, didn't they?" Erik said.

"They won't bother transporting us. They'll torch this place with us in it before the Russians can even attempt to liberate us."

The men continued to argue. Aarne considered the possibility of an evacuation. There were so many ill and in the hospital. Too many were weak from starvation or dying from the latest outbreak of disease. Winter was fast approaching. Evacuation was a deadly option, but so was the SS shooting the prisoners before the Russians arrived.

Aarne stared wide-eyed at the sailors. He didn't know what to believe. How and when he would reach freedom, he could not guess. He needed only to live day by day, hour by hour, determined to survive with whatever means possible. Those who had once bombed his hometown during the Winter War and fought his brothers in the Continuation War were now his only hope for freedom.

CHAPTER 9

Stutthof, Christmas 1944

—〰—

HUNGER SETTLED IN AARNE'S stomach like an unwanted visitor. Like the other starving prisoners, he scavenged for food bits wherever possible, stealing it from the camp stores, garden plots, workplaces, and trash dumps. Anything was fair game, whether edible or not. Every day he saw emaciated prisoners foraging for food scraps, eating plants and roots and even unpalatable items like carpenter glue and axle grease.

Those who managed to catch a stray cat or dog or steal an SS rabbit were amongst the lucky. There were even rumours there had once been a swan in the pond in front of the command building, but some fortunate prisoners had caught and eaten it. Aarne wondered what it had tasted like.

He glanced around the barrack as he tidied his bed. His warm breath hung in the cold air, and the windows were frosted around the edges. Winter would soon arrive.

What will become of these men? he wondered as he looked at the once vibrant sailors, their faces drawn and pale. Their formerly bright eyes looked lifeless, betraying their despair. Hunger and thirst were constant companions.

"Hey, look," Kalevi said. "It's snowing."

Something about the fresh, white flakes falling against the slate sky made Aarne smile. The men seemed to revive as they pulled themselves to look out the window.

"It's going to be a white Christmas," someone said from the corner bunk, a note of sarcasm in his voice.

"Maybe not a merry Christmas, but snow means water. Fresh water."

Finding clean water was a challenge. Although the camp was surrounded by water, the Baltic Coast only three kilometres north, Vistula River to the west, and Vistula Bay and a web of channels to the south and east, the poor quality from the marshy area exacerbated the ill health of the inmates.

Aarne relied on his rations of coffee and soup, knowing that the well water was unhealthy to drink. But it wasn't enough to stave off dehydration, especially with the demands of his daily duties.

The men gathered whatever bowls or cups they could find and ran outside. Despite the chilly air, they gathered bits of snow and brought it inside to melt. Some made snowballs to suck on, rejoicing in the fresh, icy water.

Aarne downed his water, watching as the flakes fell to the ground outside. Christmas was approaching. He wondered if he would make it that long.

—⚉—

Aarne bundled his clothes around his body, hoping to seal the draft that entered from his wrists and slid under his jacket. Aarne's summer clothes consisted of a shirt, a lightweight jacket, and a light-coloured pair of trousers. The other Finnish sailors still wore the clothes they were arrested in while some of the Norwegian policeman wore old Italian army uniforms they had been issued on arrival. He noticed that many prisoners stuffed newspaper or cement-bag paper under their jackets as extra layers of protection, but the punishment if discovered was severe: several lashings by the guards. He didn't want to risk it.

With the harvest in, Aarne began working around the main camp, pushing a wooden delivery cart between the camp buildings. Stutthof was much larger than he had originally realized. The new camp, forty wooden huts in four rows of ten each, was north of the old camp and housed most of the new inmates, including the overflowing population of Jewish prisoners. To the west were six huts for German and Hungarian prisoners, also called Sonderlager, inaccessible behind its own electrified fence. It was rumoured that some of them had been arrested for making an attempt on Hitler's life.

There was also a brick guardhouse for the SS, garages, dog kennels, pigsties, stables, and cages for Angora rabbits. A utility building with stores, disinfection chambers, baths, and a kitchen were also located in the new camp. DAW workshops where many of Aarne's shipmates worked used ten of the new camp's huts on the eastern side. Frequently Aarne delivered materials to the workshops or transported fabricated items to the train.

One day, as he pushed and pulled the heavy cart, he observed inmates of every age, colour, and national identity. The guard prodded them to keep moving; as they did Aarne overheard conversations in many tongues, and he wondered why all of these people were there. What had they done? Were they criminals? Were they like him, stolen from their work and homes?

He couldn't help but notice that many of the prisoners were dressed in the camp-issued clothes. On most the once blue-and-white stripes of the shirt, hat, and pants looked brown and faded. Holes and rips were common, and the clothes looked ragged and worn in spots. Some people wore clothes several sizes too large while others' were far too small. They wore what they were issued since they had given up all possessions when they had arrived at the camp. Some, Aarne learned, had been there for several years, wearing the same worn camp clothes with little opportunity to change or wash them.

"What are they wearing on their feet?" Aarne asked. The man pushing the cart beside him glanced around.

"*Klompen*. You know, wooden shoes," the man whispered, trying not to catch the attention of the SS man.

The uncomfortable-looking shoes were slightly moulded on top and bottom. Snow and mud stuck to their bases. Some prisoners looked like they would trip, their shoes too large for their bare feet. Others had their feet squeezed in and their heels jutting out. *It would be impossible to run in them*, Aarne thought.

"I've seen them before," he said. "I'm sure we transported them on the *Wappu* to Germany and Poland. I think they were made in Finland." He paused. "I thought they were for factory workers." Aarne looked at the prisoners with dismay.

His own feet were sore and blistered, and his shoes cracked and tattered. But his feet were covered, unlike those who were subjected to the klompen. He could see that the wooden shoes made daily tasks even more difficult for the prisoners who were forced to wear them. Over time the wood soaked up the moisture from the swampy ground, leaving the feet to rot. The snow collected on the bottoms of the shoes, keeping them from drying, and the wood provided no warmth at all.

"I had no idea," he said. He looked away, shaking his head with deep sadness and confusion.

—◊—

A few days later, Aarne sat at the edge of his bed, leaning down to tie what was left of his frayed shoelaces. The leather soles were worn through, leaving his feet exposed to the hard, cold ground. Their once polished lustre had faded and scratched. The temperature was quickly dropping; he knew his shoes provided little defence against the snow. Some prisoners were already beginning to wrap their feet in paper or rags to keep them warm and protected. But after seeing the klompen, Aarne was thankful to have any shoes at all.

A couple of Finnish sailors hurried into the barrack. Beneath their clothes they had something large concealed.

"Where did you get those?" Aarne asked. His eyes widened as he surveyed the gleaming jackboots in the style of the Nazi soldiers'.

"We were cleaning the huts and found them. So we took them." His friend grinned. "Here, Aarne. You need these the most." He tossed the boots in Aarne's direction.

"Kiitos," he said. "But what about you?"

"No worries. I have my own." The man produced a second pair and laughed.

Aarne beamed. He kicked off his old leather shoes and pulled on the tall, black boots. They looked new. Too new.

"If the guards see me in them, I'm sure to get a beating," he said. "Or worse. There's no way I'll get away with this." He looked around at the others.

"They definitely look stolen," said Kalevi, nodding in agreement.

"Don't worry. We'll make them look like you've been wearing them the whole time."

The men gathered dirt and soot from the little stove, and Aarne took to scuffing up the leather until the boots looked like they'd spent months in the camp. They couldn't have arrived at a better time: the smell of winter gusted through the barrack doors whenever they opened and seeped through the cracks in the wall like fog creeping silently over a field. Patches of an earlier snowfall dotted the landscape.

Aarne kept working on making the new boots look old. Although he didn't know it yet, one day those boots would save his life.

Rumours that the Finnish sailors were infested with lice ran rampant through the Scandinavian barracks. Until then the Norwegian policemen had been able to keep outbreaks under control. Now, with the Finnish sailors adding to the numbers in their camp, fear of disease intensified.

Lice meant typhus.

Typhus meant death.

The parasitic insects fed on the blood of their victims, carrying fever and typhus. The crowded conditions of the blocks meant that bugs spread rapidly throughout the camp, and as it travelled the SS crew worried it might pass into the guards' and officers' quarters. Aarne had seen the signs many times: a rash radiating from the centre of the body; a fever that lasted for weeks; and joint, back, abdomen, and head pain accompanied by nausea and vomiting. In November a typhus epidemic devastated the main camp, killing more than a thousand inmates. Outbreaks of typhus caused fear to flood the camp, and lice became the only common enemy.

One morning Aarne and his bunkmates were in the barrack when a group of SS men stormed in, yelling at them to get up and march.

"Everyone line up," a guard commanded. "Get into your rows."

Aarne looked at his shipmates. "What's happening?" he whispered, fearing the worst.

"I have no idea," said Kalevi. His face turned white and his eyes looked huge.

The men paraded into the main camp, past the long rows of barracks and the infirmary until they reached the red brick gas chamber. It was about eight and a half by three and a half metres and two and a half metres tall. There they waited for instructions from the guards.

"That's where they gas the prisoners," one of the Finns said. "I heard they fill the chamber, seal the doors, and pour in Zyklon B. They don't stand a chance."

Aarne shuddered. The guards were talking amongst themselves.

"The crematory," the man continued, nodding in the direction of the larger building behind them. "A prisoner piles the bodies in the oven, maybe ten or eleven at time, until all that's left is ashes."

Aarne stood in silence, watching the smoke rise from the eighteen-metre-tall chimney. It seemed to be in constant use. Pale, thin, naked bodies were piled like matchsticks, several high beside the crematory, awaiting their dreadful fate. Aarne began to shake. Why were they there?

Finally a guard gave the orders. "Take off your clothes."

Aarne fumbled with the buttons on his shirt. He couldn't control his quaking. The air stung his flesh. The others stood around him, shivering from the elements or perhaps from fear.

Aarne watched silently as the lice-infested clothes were collected. What would the guards do with them?

The clothes were deposited into the small chamber. The doors were latched shut.

Aarne continued to shiver but felt a sudden sense of relief. *Better my clothes than me*, he thought grimly, glancing at the sunken faces of the dead along the crematory walls. As the helpless, naked victims stood quivering outside the gas chamber, waiting for the fumes to eradicate the vile creatures, the guards began to throw abuse.

"You foul creatures. You pigs," one said as he swung his baton, his blows landing squarely against a sailor's shrunken body.

Aarne kept his eyes down, his feet planted on the earth. The cold crept up his legs. Finally the guards took the clothes from the gas chamber and threw them back at the sailors. Aarne rummaged to find his.

"Mine still have lice," an inmate said, picking a creature off between his thumb and forefinger. "It didn't work."

"It didn't work, you say?" A guard turned his rage at the offender. He flew into a fury. He pummelled the prisoner with blows until he dropped to the ground.

"Any more complaints?" asked the guard, his face red with anger, sweat dripping from his brow. The sailor lay helpless at his feet. "No? Good. Get back to your barrack." The guard stepped over the prisoner, barely missing his body with the heel of his jackboot.

Aarne fell in line behind his column. He took one last look at the crematory, the smoke spiralling up towards heaven. He remembered the greeting they had received from an officer on their arrival in Stutthof, after the death gate had opened: "There is only one way out, and that is to fly out through the chimney."

Work on the delivery crew meant Aarne spent much of his day in the main camp, transporting materials between the narrow-gauge railroad stop located behind the crematory and gas chamber and various buildings in the camp.

Six prisoners pushed the wooden wagon, with its big bar for steering and large, rubber tires, while guards walked on either side and another behind, watching the prisoners' every move. Mostly Aarne did not know what they were transporting. The boxes from the workshops were generally fairly light and may have contained some metal parts for the plane factory. Sometimes they delivered tools and other materials to the workshops or the DAW factory. Days and days passed as the crew pushed the wagon back and forth over the uneven, often muddy ground. As the temperatures dipped, the ground froze in uneven ridges.

One day the wagon crew was transferring supplies from the train to the SS kitchen in the command building. The four-winged, red brick building had impressed Aarne when he had first arrived. On special occasions or when dignitaries were visiting, two-storey-high Nazi flags with their striking black, white, and red swastika designs flanked the sides of the structure. Kalevi had been right. No prisoners entered the place unless they were working. It held only offices, officers' quarters, and visitor rooms.

As Aarne carried boxes of food from the cart through the halls of the command building, he passed several SS men dressed in clean and pressed uniforms, but he avoided eye contact. He deposited the boxes into the SS kitchen, inhaling the aromas and eyeing the fresh vegetables and fruit. He felt the eyes of the guards boring into him. It was virtually impossible to steal anything with the burly armed guards nearby.

Furtively he looked for an opportunity to pocket some food, knowing the consequences for stealing were extremely harsh: public beatings or execution were not uncommon.

The last time he had stolen something was several years before. Aarne, Matti, and Kauko had known they shouldn't even have been there. The boys had allowed the gentle current of the idyllic channel to glide them lazily through the water until they had approached the house of the Åström leather factory's head engineer. Aarne looked up as he took long, quiet strokes, admiring the building. It was a lovely place, larger than most by Oulu standards.

He glanced up at the balcony overlooking the water and scanned the grounds to ensure they were undetected. With strong strokes he swam to shore and pulled himself up on the muddy bank before ducking stealthily through the grounds. In the engineer's garden, surrounded by pink and white pennycress and purple bellflowers, the boys spread themselves out around the bushes and picked the engineer's ripe, red strawberries. The sun spread its warmth on their tanned bodies as they ate to their hearts' content.

Aarne looked up when he heard the clopping of footsteps moving across the wooden planks on the veranda above them.

"Up there. Do you see him?" Aarne lowered his head and tried to sink into the ground.

"He's got a gun," Matti almost shouted.

"Shhh." Aarne looked up to see if the engineer had spotted them.

The man slowly raised his .22 rifle and pointed it directly at the three young boys cowering behind the bushes.

"What are you doing in my garden?" the engineer's deep voice demanded.

"Let's get out of here," Aarne said. He popped his remaining strawberry into his mouth and chewed as he stooped towards the water.

"I'm right behind you," Matti replied as he followed Aarne and Kauko, head and shoulders ducked low to avoid exposure.

The three boys scurried from the garden, lips reddened by the sweet juice of the strawberries as they dove into the channel. The trigger clicked back, and a small splash hit the water a few feet from Aarne. Another shot resounded through the air. The bullet zipped into the water, leaving behind small, circular ripples. With all their strength, the boys drew themselves across the river, their feet a storm of splashes as they dodged the engineer's anger. After several metres, safely out of the enemy's sight, the boys slowed their strokes and paddled to the shoreline, where they waded to the riverbank, flopped on land, and laughed with delight.

Those days seemed like a pleasant dream from long ago, and now he was living in a nightmare. Hunger often trumped his fear of punishment. He salivated at the sight of the kitchen's food, but this time, he realized, stealing wasn't possible. He sighed and turned away. Perhaps next time he would have better luck.

—⚍—

Aarne struggled with a heavy load as he walked down a long corridor of a string of barracks in the old camp, trying to see inside the various rooms off the main hallway. Through an open door he glimpsed the *Häftlings-Krankenbau*, the inmates' infirmary, where several people lay motionless. The sight was depressing. He couldn't imagine they would ever have the strength to leave this place.

Beside the infirmary, an open door led into what looked to be an operating room with a metal surgical table. He paused to take a closer look. The table had thick sides and a thin bottom, with a hole in the centre. The metal bottom sloped towards the hole, so a patient's blood could run down into the buckets below. Various medical utensils were on a tray near the table. A small sink was attached to the wall.

Aarne turned away from the sparse room in dread and continued down the corridor. He had heard about the sick being sent to the camp hospital, the *Revier*, and never returning. Inmates who worked in the hospital said the very sick were often injected with phenol, hastening their deaths. After that, every time he passed the infirmary he walked more quickly and hastily looked away.

Fortunately Aarne was never sent to the Revier, but the stories he heard around the camp instilled a fear of the hospital and its staff. In this place death prowled in every corner. It loitered in the potato fields, in the workshops, and on the freight trains. It stalked the huts at night, lurked behind the eyes of the guards, and stood at attention in the roll call square. It was a sip of water, a beating, a phenol injection, and a Zyklon B pellet. Death was only vaguely veiled, and Aarne was determined to elude it.

—⚍—

As desperation set in, the Finnish prisoners began to notice that items in their block were disappearing.

"But who could it be?" Aarne asked. "Why would any of us steal from our own?"

"I can't understand it," Kalevi said. "Maybe it's one of the guards or another prisoner sneaking in."

After several days things continued to go missing. Aarne noticed the sailors began to watch one another with suspicion, and everyone took extra precautions with their few personal items. Stealing in the camp was commonplace, but to take from fellow block members outraged the Finnish sailors. Finally the men gathered together to discuss the situation.

Aarne sat at the edge of his bunk, his back hunched so as not to hit the bunk above.

"We must find out who is responsible for the stolen items," one of the sailors said.

"He must be reprimanded," said another.

"Who will punish him if we catch him?"

No one volunteered. Some looked at each other. Others stared at their feet.

"We will all take responsibility for punishing the burglar, so it doesn't rest on the shoulders of only one man," said the first sailor. "We must all agree, and everyone must take part, without exception." He looked around the room with steely blue eyes.

The sailors contemplated his words and nodded in silent agreement. It was the only way.

Surveillance began. After a few days, the men caught the suspect trying to take an item from under a bunk. Aarne heard him plead with his captor, begging not to be reprimanded. The sailors agreed upon the punishment and unwillingly began preparations.

They tied the man to a long, wooden table. Aarne watched in horror. The thief did not struggle. Another man produced a leather belt. He stood in readiness over his fellow sailor, his face expressionless.

The thief waited silently, closing his eyes. He clenched his hands into fists.

Aarne held his breath. The first blow struck. The sailor's body tensed, but he did not cry out. His knuckles whitened.

Aarne watched in dread as one by one the sailors struck the man on his back. Red lines welled up, a kind of angular crosshatch pattern emerging on his skin.

When it was his turn, Aarne gripped the belt. He walked up to the table. He paused. He avoided looking at the man's face. With a deep breath, he raised his hand. Closing his eyes he let the belt fly, hearing the sound as it slapped against the skin. His arm slackened.

Aarne hung his head and turned away. His eyes stung, and his hands shook as he passed the belt to the next man.

By the end the sailor was left exhausted and in pain, the signs of his punishment crisscrossing his back. After the incident there was no more stealing amongst the Finnish sailors.

Daily life for Aarne came to have a regular if gruesome routine: rations, work, threats, sleep, illness, death. Every night people died of illness and starvation. Every morning, while Aarne worked in the camp, he saw the dead collected on a cart. Their clothes were removed, and their bodies were tossed on the wooden wagon for delivery to the crematory. It could not keep up with the numbers and burned down. A funeral pyre was erected in the forest outside the camp to dispose of the thousands of bodies. Aarne could sometimes see the trail of smoke rise from the pines.

The Finns tried their best to stay healthy, relying on one another in times of physical illness and mental distress. Against the odds Aarne continued to survive the harsh camp conditions, eluding that ultimate thief: death.

CHAPTER 10

Letter Home, January 1945

—⁓—

WINTRY AIR SWOOPED OVER the camp and wrapped its arms securely around the barracks, settling in for a long visit. As December slowly
inched to the end of the year, Aarne could see the conditions in the

camp continue to deteriorate. Disease, especially typhus, was decimating the population. The frozen corpses outside the crematory were piled high. Hunger and hard labour made life unbearable, and fear of abuse and beatings was a constant stressor. Visions of home haunted Aarne's dark hours.

One night, as he drifted in and out of a fitful sleep, he pictured his mother's face, her dark hair pulled up in a bun at the nape of her neck. The soft sound of her voice was a distant memory. He tried to close his eyes and hear it, but it seemed so faint, so far away. If only he could tell her that he was still alive.

"I'm all right, Äiti," he whispered to the air as he floated in sleep. "I'll be fine." His mother smiled at him. He tried to reach out to touch her, but she faded away.

Somewhere far away Anna Liisa dreamed of her lost son. She hadn't heard from him in so long and didn't know where he was or if he was still alive. In her vision he was smiling his broad grin, healthy and happy, like the young man who had so bravely left his hometown on a train to Helsinki.

—⟶

The Finnish detainees were called together for a meeting. An official dressed in a dark suit, with SS men accompanying him, strode towards them. He paused before the men, his smile fading as he took in the scene. Aarne could see the stranger struggled to maintain his pleasant expression at the sight of the dishevelled men.

"Hello," he said in Finnish. "Greetings from your home country."

Aarne's jaw dropped. This man spoke Finnish. Was he here to take them home?

"I understand that you men have been in Stutthof for many months," he said. "I have a proposal. One that I believe will be the difference between life and death for some of you."

The visitor explained that he was a Finnish statesman from Helsinki. Aarne listened intently. For the first time, he felt a glimmer of hope. The man explained his purpose.

"After you have performed your duties for the German government, you will be returned to Finland," he promised.

"But what do we have to do?" asked one of the men.

"I cannot provide you with the details. However, rest assured that you will be compensated."

Aarne observed his shipmates. By then they were in varying states of physical and mental desperation. One of the men had married just before they had sailed on their fateful trip to Poland and hadn't seen his bride in many months. All the sailors had families waiting for them at home. Aarne thought about his own mother and father and how frightened they had to be feeling.

Aarne considered the options carefully. If he went with this official, what would he be expected to do? It was clear he would be working on behalf of the Nazis, the very people who had imprisoned him and his shipmates. The very ones who treated them like animals. If he stayed his fate was unknown. Perhaps only death remained.

"Well, who would like the opportunity to leave this place?" His pen was poised over a notepad.

A few men raised their hands. The idea of leaving Stutthof was enough for them to agree to the statesman's uncertain terms. Aarne could understand their decision. It might mean they would save their own lives.

The official smiled and wrote down names, nodding his head as he spoke to each man in turn. The other men held back, arms crossed in defiance. A few walked away. Most of the sailors, like Aarne, refused to take the deal. He wanted nothing to do with working for the German government. As he returned to the barrack, he paused to look at the small group standing around the statesman. Was he making the right decision? Would he ever see home again?

—〰—

As winter's grip embraced the camp in a death hold, the sounds of gunfire volleyed back and forth, low-flying planes droned above, and explosions echoed closer and closer to the camp. By January the rumours of liberation escalated through the barracks. Much of the news was unreliable. Some of the information was from inmates who worked in the camp administration offices, who had regular access to the German newspapers or overheard reports on the radio. They delivered information back to their blocks, and it moved rapidly from person to person. Some deliberately passed along positive, overly optimistic reports in order to lift spirits, leaving out the information that might create more tension. However any news from the outside world provided Aarne with a sense that a different life could exist, and the war would eventually end.

These days Aarne's mind often turned towards home. What was his family thinking? Did they believe his ship had been attacked at sea? Perhaps they believed it had encountered a mine or was disabled on some distant shore. Did they know that the Germans had captured the crew?

One night his brother, Kalle, had a dream about his lost sibling. In it he saw Aarne aboard a tempest-tossed ship. In later years he would describe his vision to Aarne in detail:

> Dark clouds rolled across the sky as the ship was pitched like a toy in a whirlpool. Slowly it tilted and began to sink into the dark depths. Lightning blasted and momentarily lit the night sky with the flash of a lightbulb, illuminating a long pier jutting from a stretch of white sand.

A solitary figure bobbed up and down with the giant waves. His long arms flung out of the water as he attempted to swim against the powerful maelstrom. Despite the whitecaps, the young man swam to the pier, gripped the jetty, and climbed to the safety of the surface. Exhausted, he lay flat on his belly, arms to his sides, struggling for each breath.

Eventually, with the waves still crashing behind him, the wind howling against his drenched clothes, and the thunder roaring in the distance, he gathered what little strength remained. With one hand planted on the deck, the other on his thigh, he struggled to his knees and then to his feet. He stumbled down the pier, towards the beach, head lowered against the raging wind. With each step his body gained power. By the time he reached the white sands, his strength was renewed, and he strode confidently into the distance. The storm abated as the sun slowly peered through the dark clouds.

The dream reassured Kalle, and he shared it with his family, believing it meant Aarne would return home safely.

Aarne clung to his own visions and the memories of his family, just as they believed that their imaginings foretold a happier future for their lost son. With only their dreams to hold on to, Aarne and his family alike hoped for his safe return from the distant shore upon which he had landed.

—⁂—

It was early January. The cold wind whipped through the barracks, and snow blanketed the bleak camp. The tall pines were laced with white trim, and the sun made a feeble effort to peer through the grey clouds.

Aarne crossed his arms over his chest, hunching his shoulders as he tried to keep warm. He sat across from a Swedish translator at a long, wooden table in one of the huts. The older man held a pen over a fresh sheet of lined paper.

"But what should I say?" Aarne asked. Almost three months after his imprisonment, he was finally allowed to write a letter home to his family. "Where do I begin?"

"Just begin, Aarne," the translator said in Finnish. "But remember that the SS will surely read it and censor anything negative."

"Why can't I write it myself?" he asked.

"There are no guards or officers who can read and understand Finnish here," the translator explained. "Just tell me in Finnish, I'll write in Swedish, and someone will read it over before sending it off."

Aarne nodded. As he contemplated what to say, he rolled a piece of paper between his fingers. He imagined telling them about the *Wappu*'s arrival in Danzig. He thought about being detained in port, the empty warehouse, and the enclosed dance hall. He shuddered as he remembered the cattle car, the long train trip, the first sight of Stutthof. He shook his head. He saw himself gathering wood around camp, labouring in the potato fields, pushing the delivery cart. He envisioned Stutthof's detainees, the dying, and the dead.

"How can I tell them everything that's happened? How can I tell them where I am?" He looked up at the translator, who waited patiently.

"You don't tell them everything. Say that you are well," the translator said. "That's what they want to hear."

Aarne had felt happy about the prospect of writing home, but now he frowned, digging his fists under his arms, his right knee bobbing up and down under the table. He had often wondered how his parents and siblings were doing. Had they received news about his whereabouts? Had they learned that the *Wappu* had been captured? Did they know he was in a concentration camp? Perhaps they already believed he was dead. A letter home would let them know he was in Poland. Memories of home rushed forward like water being released in a canal; the locks he had tried to create in his mind had kept his thoughts contained for only so long.

"Just tell me what you want to write, and I'll put it down in Swedish," the translator said. On the top right corner, he wrote the sender's name and address: "Aarne Kovala of Sonderlagen, Stutthof, Danzig, Germany." Below he wrote the date: "10-1-45." On the top right, the scribe wrote the addressee's information: "Juho Kovala, Oulu, Sähkölaitos Finland."

Aarne hesitated, considering all of his options.

"You can't tell them too much, or the camp authorities won't send your letter," the translator suggested. "Let them know you are well. Ask for care packages."

The idea of Red Cross parcels buoyed his spirits. Several times before, Aarne had benefitted from the care packages of others. When he had received a gift of smoked salmon from one of the Norwegians, he had been extremely grateful. He hadn't tasted anything so good in many months. The fish reminded him of Oulu, where salmon regularly swam through the rapids of the Oulujoki. Others in Stutthof also received items, although much of what they received ended up in the hands of the camp authorities. Goods were used to bribe the guards or trade with other inmates. Perhaps if his parents would be able to send items, he and his crewmates could use them and maybe help some of the others as well.

Aarne started dictating his letter a few times and then stopped. He tried again, wanting to get the words just right. It was so difficult to think his family would read this letter, yet he could really say nothing about the truth of this place. If nothing else he was relieved that his parents would learn of his fate: he was alive. For now.

Dear Pappa!

Greetings from here, far away! I have been healthy and feeling well and wish the same for you. We may now write a few lines in Swedish, but we do not know when we may write again. From there you may write as often as you wish and send packages. Find out from Finland's Red Cross or direct through the Swedish Red Cross. Write replies in Swedish and write on the envelope Schwedishe Sprache in the corner. Don't send any clothes but neither such [things] that will be destroyed or spoiled if they lie for a long time. I hope the day soon dawns when we again may meet.

Greetings to all acquaintances and friends. Many, many greetings to you all there at home.

Aarne

When the letter was done, the translator put his pen down. Aarne sighed.

"It's a good letter, Aarne," he said.

Aarne nodded. "At least they will know where I am and that I'm alive."

The translator copied the address on the envelope, carefully folded the letter, and placed it in an envelope. Aarne watched as he put it on the pile with the others, ready for the administration to survey it, stamp it in red with the Nazi insignia, and send it out in the post more than a month later. He wondered if his parents would ever see it. In fact they did not receive the letter until the summer of 1945—much too late for them to learn about their son's fate during the war.

—⚉—

Two days after writing the letter, unbeknownst to Aarne, the Red Army's winter offensive began, and civilians started to evacuate the region. The formal order for the evacuation of Stutthof Camp was given on January 23, 1945.

Although Aarne hoped the end of the war was approaching, he also feared that the front lines were getting too close to the camp. There was no chance the Germans would give them up easily. Aarne heard rumours the camp would be vacated, but this was a scenario that could be devastating for the weakened and sick inmates. Even more frightening and disturbing was the alternative: mass execution. He had heard rumours that Himmler had commanded the SS to ensure no prisoner was left alive for the advancing troops. That meant either departure or death.

As the Russian front lines advanced towards the camp, Aarne's fear escalated. The atmosphere in the barracks was tense. Aarne noticed that the SS crew was on high alert and posted extra guards around the camp, constantly vigilant. Some prisoners formed resistance groups and began preparing by scrounging for extra food and clothes. By January 20, kommandos left their regular employment in order to begin preparing materials for evacuation. The SS staff worked furiously to destory camp records, especially hospital and political department documents, while groups of inmates packed other camp files. Machinery and equipment were disassembled and shipped away.

On the morning of January 25, 1945, Commandant Paul Werner Hoppe issued the order at five o'clock. Evacuation of the camp began an hour later. It would be one more day before Aarne and the other Finns would be forced to leave, unaware of what the next several weeks held in store for them as they started the infamous death march.

CHAPTER 11
Death March, January 1945

———⚍———

AARNE AWOKE TO THE familiar barking of German guards at three o'clock in the morning. It was January 26, the second day of evacuation.

Today he would be departing the camp, like seven columns of about nine thousand people had done the day before. He did not know where they were going or how long they would be marching as he'd watched them line up in columns of five with the inmates from their individual huts. The guards conducted the roll call before marching them out of the gates on that cold morning, leaving behind those too sick or disabled to walk. In the end, of the approximately twenty-four thousand inmates, almost half of the prisoners would be leaving the camp. Many looked too ill to march but feared what would happen if they stayed behind, so they took their chances. There were still many left, and Aarne knew his group would be next.

Still in the darkness of predawn, 121 Norwegians and Finns gathered in the roll call square. They were joined by 700 Polish, Jewish, Russian and French people from the main camp. Aarne looked around. It was a smaller contingent than yesterday's group. Only the women were left, about 1,600 of them, and the sick or dying. The women were scheduled to leave the camp later that morning. Aarne didn't know the fate of those who would remain. He feared the worst. As he contemplated their chances, the wind whipped through the air, and snow whirled around his legs.

Aarne waited in line, bundling his jacket around his body, thankful for the stolen SS boots he had received earlier that fall. They didn't fit quite right, but they were warm and protected his feet. Others weren't so lucky.

The guards took roll call. The longer Aarne stood, the stiffer his legs became. The wind howled. The guards bellowed orders. The inmates waited.

Two days of rations were handed out: 500 grams of bread and 120 grams of margarine. Aarne watched a few of the famished inmates immediately devour their meagre rations, leaving nothing for the long days ahead. He took his and carefully placed it in a pocket. It wasn't much. *Perhaps the journey would be short*, he thought. *Perhaps not.*

Aarne shivered at the prospect of leaving the camp in the dead of winter. How would these bodies that surrounded him, already bone thin and weary, manage to trudge through the thick snow and raw wind? How could he?

By half past three o'clock, still in the dark, column eight was marching, five prisoners in each row. The morning was bitter. After several hours of slogging through the snow, Aarne saw the sun begin to peek through the pine trees, a pale glow of yellow and pink over the blue-grey snow. Briefly he closed his eyes, hoping the scant sun would warm his face as his body shivered. It did little to heat him, but the dim daylight drove him forward. Before him a man's hunched shoulders; on either side the dragging arms of his crewmates. Behind him the sound of footsteps crunching on the snow, always at his heels, spurred him on. Step after step he kept trudging.

Aarne focused on the road ahead, only occasionally glimpsing the landscape. The pristine snow stretched across the sloping fields and curving roads, capping the branches of the bare trees and dripping from the pines along the route. The early morning light became a haze behind grey clouds as the snow began to fall. The temperature plummeted. Snowflakes swirled, slapping Aarne's face, stinging his eyes and biting his nose. It was another assault on his already weary body.

As the snow deepened along the road, each step became more difficult. His feet were frozen in his jackboots, his legs numb from the cold. Within the first few kilometres, Aarne saw inmates along the roadside where they had fallen to the ground, unable to continue. The march was silent save for the whipping wind and the voices of the guards berating an inmate or firing a shot.

"Get up. Keep moving," a guard bellowed at a downed man. Aarne saw the victim struggle to his knees and pull himself to his feet. He rejoined the group, trying to keep up with the slow pace. Aarne knew that the man could not continue much longer. A little ways down the road, he finally succumbed to exhaustion.

Farther along he saw a form huddled at the roadside, the white and blue stripes of his clothes barely visible against the snow. One of the guards rushed forward. Aarne watched as he gave the fallen man a few hard kicks with his boots. Each strike made Aarne jolt. The prisoner barely moved. The guard pulled out his weapon. Standing over the body, he aimed. Aarne waited. He held his breath. The guard pulled the trigger.

The shot echoed through the valley. A group of birds flapped from a nearby tree. The snow from the branches fell in a mass, leaving indentations on the ground below. Soon they would be covered over, like the bodies left on the roadside.

No one spoke. It took all of Aarne's energy to keep moving one foot in front of the other. Sometimes he heard the guards yelling at stragglers. Often the guards hit them from behind with their rifle butts. The blows sent some face first into the snow, where they would remain motionless. Once in a while, he heard the whimpers or groans of bodies lying on the road. Most were silent.

—〰—

The planned evacuation route brought the group west from Stutthof through Neckelswalde to the Vistula, a wide river that fed into the Baltic. As Aarne's column approached, he noticed a large boat attached to a cable across the expanse. It was filled with people. Large chunks of ice floated downriver with the current, crunching against one another, wrestling briefly before shifting and moving again.

Eying the frozen river, Aarne waited. He feared the barge was going to get wedged between the travelling sheets of ice or capsize in the frigid water. As he stood at the edge of the waterway, waiting to be transferred across, he huddled with his group, shrinking his cold body into his clothing and wrapping his arms around his torso. The northerly wind whipped across his face. Sticking his chin into his jacket and his shoulders up against his ears, he stamped his feet to keep from freezing on the spot.

"We'll never make it," he mumbled, shaking his head at the prospect of the crossing. Before, he had convinced himself he had to keep going.

Now he had his doubts. This might be the end. Aarne looked around him. Rows and rows of hundreds of prisoners waited for the solitary barge. On the other side, those who had safely made it across the moving ice fields were already departing for the next leg of the journey.

"We'll make it," Kalevi said, reading Aarne's expression. "We're not done yet."

"Not everyone will," Aarne said, pointing to the side of the path.

Several inmates, fallen in the snow, their bodies contorted like grotesque statues, had frozen while they waited. A thin layer of snow was already beginning to cover their nameless features. Aarne's gaze returned to the vessel. It was useless to consider the destinies of those he passed. If he did so, he feared, his own will to survive would slide away.

Once on board, Aarne stood stationary, hoping for safe transport over the freezing depths. The wind whistled as the vessel crunched through the ice, the water lapping its sides hungrily, ready to pounce and devour them should it capsize.

A large sheet of ice flowed towards the open barge. Aarne watched as it glided towards him. He held his breath. The boat kept its steady pace. The ice shifted in one direction and then the other. He tracked it until it slipped past. He breathed a sigh of relief.

Finally they reached the other shore. Ahead was a long, flat road in an open space. Rows of dark figures plodding through the snow already dotted the way ahead. He could see that the expanse provided no shelter from the bitter elements. Once again he was filled with dread.

There is no way anyone can stand this for very long, Aarne thought as the wind made the snow circle and whirl around him in a wintery typhoon.

They began to tramp again through the deepening drift. He could see the despair written on the faces around him. Those who could no longer walk gave up and sat down on the path, heads slumped between their knees, knowing the guards would surely kick them to death, shoot them on the spot, or leave them to freeze. He watched, confused, as another inmate accosted a fallen prisoner who was too weak to protest.

Then he realized. The shoes. He wanted the shoes. Sometimes he saw people taking clothing from the fallen, but many were too frozen to allow for such pilfering.

By the end of the first day, having covered more than twenty kilometres, the column passed through a village, and by nightfall they reached a farm. Aarne could hear the exchange of gunfire in the distance. The front line was so close, the farmers had already abandoned their homes, taking with them whatever they could manage.

The detainees were herded into a barn for the first night. It was teeming with tired bodies, all searching for dry places to sleep on the scant hay scattered over the hard floor. Eventually Aarne found a place to lie down. He huddled between his shipmates, grateful to have some shelter from the wind that shrilled in through the cracks of the wooden boards. Exhaustion led him to a fitful sleep filled with confusing images of snow and bodies and guns. Just as he was dozing off, he was jolted by the imagined sounds of screaming and gunfire.

The next morning Aarne awoke to begin another long day of marching. Many others, however, did not: they had frozen solid in the night.

Hunger continued to plague him. He had already consumed what little rations he had received on the morning of the evacuation. Most of the others were in the same condition or worse. He noticed with envy a man eating something he discreetly pulled from his pocket, avoiding the attention of his hungry companions. If he was discovered someone would surely steal the food. It was difficult to believe that the conditions could be worse now than they had been at the camp. They were.

Aarne fell into line beside his shipmates. The Finnish sailors tried to stay together during the entire march, bolstering one another to continue.

"Wait for me," an Estonian man said to the group of Finns as they began to file into rows.

Aarne looked up. He had spoken to this man many times at the camp. During the march Aarne had often noticed him walking alongside the Finns.

The man was having trouble. He struggled to keep up with the group, his feet dragged through the snow, and he took a few quick steps on occasion as he fell behind.

As the day wore on, Aarne's fatigue increased. Around him the others were clearly battling with the snow. His legs ached, but he pushed on. He glanced behind him, at the Estonian. He was falling farther and farther behind.

"Please...please...help me," the Estonian said, his eyes pleading. "I can't walk any longer."

"You must keep going," someone said. "Come on now."

The Finns encouraged him, but none had any strength to aid him physically. Everyone was having difficulty. After several more metres, the Estonian fell to his knees in the snow.

"Finn boys, Finn boys, help me," he said. He lifted his arm to the group, his eyes wide in desperation. His body slumped into the snow.

Aarne slowed, looking at the Estonian's scared face. He hesitated. If only he could lift him from the snow and carry him down the road. But it was impossible. He could barely keep himself standing.

The Estonian lay motionless. A German soldier came from behind the column. Aarne watched as the soldier paused over the man. He heard the thud as the soldier's black jackboot struck the side of the fallen figure. The Estonian barely responded. The German produced his pistol from its holster and aimed it at the curled figure. He clicked the trigger. Bright red blood poured from the Estonian's neck, soaking into the snow. His vacant eyes stared into the distance. He was finally free.

Aarne turned his face away and kept marching, shoulders slumped heavily. He could hear the man's voice in his head, pleading with him to help. He swept away the stream running down his cheek.

—ᴠᴠ—

Day after day Aarne's group walked and walked. A few days on, they came across a man traveling with his young son. Aarne had seen them a few times before, walking the same road as the group from Stutthof.

"Papa, I can't walk anymore," the boy said. His eyes pleaded with his father, whose own body was clearly giving out.

"Come to me," his father said, and he lifted his son into his arms.

Aarne watched the weakened man carry his son. The boy wrapped his arms around his father and burrowed his face into his neck. Each footstep seemed like a greater struggle than the last. He marvelled at the father's determination as the kilometres passed. Finally someone moved alongside the pair.

"Why don't you place your son in the back of this little sleigh?" the stranger suggested. "It will be easier for you to pull him than to carry him so far."

"Yes, I can try that," the man said with a weak smile.

The father gently placed the boy down. The sled was already packed high with provisions, but it was easier to drag the boy than carry him. The father bundled the boy under thick clothing, smiling down at the pale face and talking to him in hushed tones.

Aarne trudged, occasionally glancing over at the two. The boy lay still on the sled, the man leaning forward with his remaining strength to help move the runners through the snow. Eventually the father stopped the cart to check on his boy.

"My son...no!" the man cried as he uncovered his son's face. The little boy's wide eyes gazed blankly into the distance. His tiny body was frozen. The father sobbed quietly as he wrapped his arms around his son's lifeless body. Aarne paused as the father embraced his child, kneeling beside him in the snow.

"You must keep moving," one of the travellers said, touching the man on the shoulder.

The father shook his head, pulling his son closer to his chest. "I can't leave my little boy," he said as he rocked his child back and forth. "He is all I have left."

Aarne looked away, tears forming in his eyes. The men looked at one another and then turned towards the long row that would trudge them forward into their own uncertain future, leaving the tragic tableau of the father and child at the side of the road. The man with the sleigh shook his head and continued on without them.

As Aarne marched he wondered about the bodies he saw littered along the path. What about the families? Would they ever know how their loved ones died? Would they ever be able to retrieve their bodies, left to rot at the side of the road or buried in mass graves? Aarne shuddered.

He was determined not to be one of those unnamed bodies in an unmarked grave. Somehow he had to continue.

—⟨⟨⟩—

For days they marched with nothing. No food. No water. No warmth. No hope.

A flurry of activity startled Aarne as they entered a small village. A group of people were running away from their columns.

"Get back to your line," a soldier commanded, firing a shot towards them.

They scrambled and tripped through the snow, yelling in delight in Polish. Aarne couldn't understand the words but knew they were excited about something. He tracked their movement to a rounded brick structure with thick snow dripping from the earthen roof. A small, steel door suggested it was for cooking. The Polish prisoners had immediately recognized it as a farmer's outdoor oven.

"Open the door," a man said.

"Look! It's bread."

"Bread!"

The oven was cold, but inside were great rolls of unbaked dough. The farmers must have left in great haste to leave behind their unbaked bread. Several people grabbed sticks and attempted to get the dough out, shoving one another for even a morsel.

"Halt!" A German guard ordered. "Get back in line."

The inmates continued to push and fight one another.

"Move back to your lines. Now." The soldier commanded.

The Poles continued to ignore the orders. The soldier drew his pistol and began shooting indiscriminately. One by one the prisoners dropped to the ground beside the brick oven.

Under orders the rest continued to march forward. Aarne couldn't look at the bodies strewn beside the structure. It was too much to see their hope fallen away and their lives destroyed in one last act of desperation.

At night rest spots were seemingly chosen at random. They slept in stables, barns, farm buildings, or churches. They were forbidden to have any contact with the local inhabitants, but most people had already abandoned their homes and farms. Every morning, when Aarne woke, he struggled for a moment to remember where he was until the fog lifted, and he reawakened to his nightmare. Some mornings he realized that many of the other men were missing. They had somehow managed to escape during the cover of night. More frequently he noticed the stiff figures left lying on the ground where they had fallen to sleep, never to awaken.

—⚭—

"What is that woman doing?" Aarne asked. By then everyone knew that leaving the column meant certain death.

They were on the outskirts of another nameless village. In the distance was a *kapliczki*, a sacred roadside shrine with a large cross protruding from a mound of rocks. The woman reached the monument, threw her hands in the air, and slumped to her knees. She pressed her palms together and lowered her head.

It didn't take long for a guard to notice she was missing from the line. He walked up behind her where she kneeled before the cross. Her small body trembled, but she did not move when the guard roared.

"Stand up and return to the column."

She remained motionless. Aarne understood. She was waiting for the inevitable. Despair had led her to make one final decision.

Without hesitation the guard removed his pistol and shot her in the back of the head. Aarne's body startled at the sound. The woman's body collapsed against the rocks.

The sound of the bullet leaving its chamber echoed against the trees in the distance, shocking all of the inmates as they marched. A group of birds nestled in a nearby tree rose into the sky, scattering towards heaven. By then Aarne was familiar with the sound of intermittent gunshots, but each time he was reminded what it meant: another would not see the end of the day, would not survive the war. Some prisoners feared that outcome. Some envied it.

—◊—

One evening the guards led them into an abandoned air hangar. Aarne noticed the wide-open space and tall ceilings. It was empty apart from the inmates. German soldiers carried in the wounded, most of them Hitler Youth, to be protected from the blowing wind.

"They must have been involved in some battle," Aarne said to his friends as they watched the young soldiers, some severely injured, coming into the hangar. "They don't even look old enough to be soldiers," he whispered. Despite their official-looking uniforms, Aarne supposed they weren't much older than he was.

"Bring some branches for these men," a guard instructed. Several prisoners gathered the branches and lay them on the concrete floor, so the soldiers would have something soft on which to lie. The inmates from Stutthof, on the other hand, spread out on the hard, cold floor.

"You." A guard pointed at Aarne. "Get water for these soldiers."

There was no medical assistance for the injured, and it didn't appear that any was expected. Eventually, Aarne found a working tap and some containers. He filled his and carried it across the hangar, careful not to spill it.

Aarne knelt beside one of the boys. He looked pale and weak.

"Drink this." Aarne didn't know if the boy understood his words. The boy stared at him with fear in his eyes but parted his lips to accept the cold liquid. The boy didn't look like he would live until morning.

Aarne moved on to provide water to some of the other soldiers, wondering how many of them had survived that long, their wounds gaping and bodies barely moving. Through the night Aarne could hear the moans of the dying boys as they bled to death on the hangar floor.

The next morning the prisoners gathered to march again. The guards abandoned the wounded Hitler Youth along with the bodies of the inmates who had not survived the night. As he left the shelter, Aarne wondered what would happen to them. Maybe medical assistance was arriving to assist the young soldiers, or perhaps they were left there to die. In death, he noticed, they all looked the same.

The weather worsened: the wind blew strongly, and the temperature plummeted. The falling snow made the land blend into the sky, the horizon an indistinguishable blur. The snow fell so thickly that their progress became painfully slow.

Exhaustion haunted Aarne. He kept his boots moving, one step after another. He knew kicks and rifle butt blows to the back would follow orders to hurry up. He understood that people who trailed behind would eventually fall to their knees, and the soldiers would shoot them. Aarne saw the striped jackets and pants of the fallen along the road, frozen into surreal shapes, with bullet holes peppering their necks and heads. There was only one alternative to marching.

After several hours of hard slogging through the snow, Aarne saw a man with a German knife lodged through his mouth and out the side of his head. The sight was horrific, like a scene from a horror movie.

How is this man still alive? Aarne wondered. The man kept moving along. His jacket gradually became saturated with blood. For many hours, as he marched, Aarne marvelled at the man's tenacity. Something compelled him to keep going. What drove him to continue while others gave up was impossible to know. By evening he was dead. Aarne felt deep sadness.

—◊◊◊—

The Stutthof prisoners were not always alone on the road. The main roads were full of civilians trying to evacuate their villages and farms. German soldiers were on the road as their Wehrmacht units retreated. Sometimes, snorting horses pulling large buggies took up most of the road, forcing the inmates into the ditch. Individuals and small family groups pushed or pulled carts overflowing with furniture and personal items, children straggling behind.

The roads were sometimes so clogged, the inmates had to wait their turn, cold and tired, on the roadside. Then Aarne would watch the faces move past, young and old, men and women, all looking tired and dishevelled. There was no laughter or happy chatter. Feet crunching the snow, wheels slushing against the lane, and the occasional tired voice calling out were the only sounds.

At other times in the day, the guards led the column off of the congested main streets. The country roads proved to be even more difficult for travelling. They were narrower and covered in thicker, less trodden snow. The tall pines and firs protected them from the wind, but little sun shone through the canopy, keeping them in semidarkness for most of the day. It didn't feel like a shortcut to Aarne as he wound in and out of the forests and countryside.

One morning, as Aarne tried to keep pace with the slow-moving line, he saw a young German soldier leaning over his motorbike, fiddling with some of the controls. As Aarne passed, the man looked up and caught his eye. Aarne looked away.

"You. Yes, you. Take this bike," the soldier commanded.

Aarne stepped away from the others and took the handlebars of the Nazi's bike. The motorcycle was heavier than it appeared.

"Follow me," the soldier commanded. "Faster, now. Move it along."

Using his limited strength, Aarne pushed the heavy motorcycle through the muddy, partially frozen farm roads, worried the German might hit or shoot him if something happened to the motorbike.

"Leave it here against this wall," the soldier said when they came across a building. Luckily for Aarne the building was only a short distance from where they started. He left the motorcycle, relieved to walk away from the Nazi. He didn't know if he had the strength left to push the bike much farther. As quickly as he could, he rejoined his column.

One evening Aarne's column stopped at a farm. There was little space left in the large barn, but he managed to find a spot. At least there was no snow under the roof, and a little bit of hay was scattered over the rough wood floor. He lowered his weary body, thankful for a bit of rest.

In the middle of the night, Aarne awakened to the sounds of crying and yelling. Someone had died in the night, and others were fighting over his clothes. Within minutes six or seven German soldiers came into the structure. One gave the order, and the others put bullets in their guns, cocked their pistols, and shot the fighting prisoners all at once. Aarne turned away. Many died instantly. He tried to close his eyes, to rest a little while, but all he could hear were cries through the night. In the morning the living marched on, leaving the dead behind.

After more than eleven days of marching, Aarne's column finally reached the evacuation camp in Lauenburg County. He had endured snowstorms, freezing temperatures, crossing the Vistula River, and travelling through the roads of such towns as Klein Zűnder, Gross Zűnder, Praust, Kahlbude, Lappin, Nestempohl, Seefeld, Suckau, and Pomietschin, covering a distance of nearly 170 kilometres.

Exhausted and in pain from his journey, Aarne was thankful to be alive when he reached the destination. He could see that the number of survivors was far less than when they had left the camp but could not know that more than a third of the prisoners had either died or escaped en route to Lauenburg County. Of the 821 people in his column, only 421 arrived at the evacuation camp.

Aarne was a survivor.

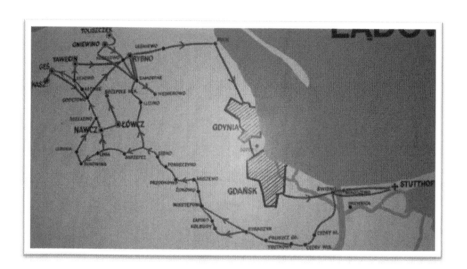

CHAPTER 12

Tauenzin Camp, February 1945

—⁂—

AARNE STAMPED HIS FEET on the bare floor as he looked around his new barrack. Column eight had stopped in Tauenzin, in Lauenburg County, taking refuge in a former summer labour camp. It was as sparse as Stutthof and was not ready for the hundreds of individuals who arrived in the middle of winter. The long days of marching across snowy roads were over, but still his heart was heavy.

He watched his breath rise in the cold air, vanishing into the rafters. The distinct smell of mould filled Aarne's nostrils as the barrack was opened for the first time in many months. No tables or benches. Bunk beds much like those he was accustomed to and a stove, if they could get it heated, to melt snow for drinkable water. Outside the water supply was easily accessible, but no water flowed from the spout. The camp was not intended to be used in the winter.

The prisoners crowded into the small, wooden huts, vying for coveted spots on the wooden bunks, but many settled for pieces of the hard floor. Aarne ran his fingertips across the dust-covered windowsills, leaving a long trail. Soon fingerprint marks dotted all the grimy surfaces. The wind snuck in through the cracks in the wall and under the door. Frost framed the edges of the glass, obscuring the view of the barrack walls next door. Behind the camp unspoiled snow covered the grounds like a fresh layer of frosting, carved into swirling patterns by the wind. Aarne sat at the edge of his bunk, his heavy head burrowed into his hands, thankful, at least, to rest his aching feet and be sheltered from the gusts that had threatened them during their long journey.

It had been days since he'd had anything to eat. He hadn't seen as much as a slice of sawdust bread in several days. He hoped now that they were in a more permanent setting, they would receive food rations, but he knew better than to dwell on it. Hope was one thing. Longing was something else. It could drive a person mad.

—⁂—

During the first few days in Tauenzin, the guards assigned the men a variety of duties around the camp. A few received assignments to the fairly well-equipped kitchen, used for serving large numbers of summer labourers. Deliveries from local farmers and activities around the camp kitchen made Aarne optimistic that food was in his future. Without it he didn't think he could last much longer.

"Line up for rations," a guard said through the door of the hut.

Even the weakest man lifted his head from his bunk at the prospect of camp gruel.

"Finally some food," Kalevi said as he and Aarne left the barrack for the short walk across the compound to the mess hall. "What do you think they'll serve us?"

"As long as it's edible, I don't care what it is," Aarne replied.

He didn't anticipate anything better than some bread and weak coffee, maybe some cold soup, but even that seemed heavenly right now.

"The Germans don't look like they have suffered from lack of food," he said, nodding in the direction of the nearest guard.

"They never go without anything, I'm sure," Kalevi said. "We're like dogs. We get the leftovers after they've had their fill."

"Their dogs probably eat better than we do." Aarne eyed a muzzled German shepherd restrained by a guard. "We get the dog's leftovers."

Weak and tired, Aarne's senses woke as the smell of soup drifted towards him. For the first time in what seemed forever, he felt a glimmer of relief as he stood in line for his rations. Each prisoner received an old metal camp bowl. He watched the steam rise as the soup poured from the ladle. With each shuffle closer to the immense pot, his mouth watered. Finally it was his turn. He held out his arms, his hands cupping the bowl with expectation. The hot liquid poured like melted gold. A few drops landed on his fingers, and he was tempted to lick them up before they fell to the ground.

Aarne enjoyed the warmth emanating from the bowl onto his frozen fingers as he found a place to hunker down with his prize. The faint smell of potatoes, turnips, and some kind of meat, perhaps horse, rose to his nostrils, and the vapours warmed his face. As he drank the tasteless soup, the insides of his mouth and throat were coated with the fluid. The watery broth travelled down, blazing a trail of heat until it filled the small space of his belly. It did not take long to be satisfied. The satiety would not last, he knew, but for now he would savour every moment.

—ᴍ—

"Look, we have to do something about this," a sailor said as he plucked at a tiny insect, squeezing it between his fingers. "We need to wash our clothes and try to drown those loathsome creatures. We don't need typhus here."

The diseases that infested Stutthof had followed them to the evacuation camps and settled into the barracks. Frostbite, diarrhoea, and typhus found new homes in Tauenzin. The huts were teeming with lice. Aarne looked down at his threadbare clothes. They hadn't been washed in ages.

"Let's fire up that stove," someone said. "We can use that empty paint can over there. Fill it with snow, and it'll melt over the heat. Then we can wash our clothes. That should kill them off."

Aarne agreed. Clean clothes were worth the effort.

One by one the inmates took turns swirling their dirt-encrusted clothes in the steaming liquid. When it was his turn, Aarne stripped down and carefully placed his clothes in the boiling water, hoping to rid them of the lice that made a home of his worn threads. With a big stick, he tried to spin the clothes in the bubbling water, using what little strength he could muster. The clothes barely moved in the pot.

"Put more effort into it, Aarne," Kalevi said.

"I'm trying," he said as he grunted.

He grabbed the stick with both hands and threw his whole body into the task. Slowly, after managing a few rotations, the clothes began to turn in a circular motion. He pulled the stick around the edge of the pot again, feeling the water gain momentum.

All of a sudden, he could feel the pot tilting. The paint can was losing its balance on the small stove. He tried to right the pot with the stick, but it was not large enough. He didn't have the strength.

As if in slow motion, the boiling liquid slanted to one side, and the pot began tipping. Before he could think about what he was doing, Aarne's arm shot out to catch it before it spilled all over the floor. The hot metal pot plummeted. Aarne's forearm took the brunt of the scorching water and searing clothes, burning his skin on contact.

"Ahhhh!" He gasped for air between screams of pain. "Help me...it stings!"

The others cried out in alarm, moving away from the boiling water as the clothes were strewn across the floor.

"Hold on, Aarne." Kalevi helped move him away from the mess. He sat on a bunk, the agony written in the lines of his contorted face.

"Wait. I think I have something to help you." One of the sailors ran to his bunk, where he had hidden a tub of ointment under the mattress.

Aarne held out his burned arm, his fingers in a white-knuckled fist, trying to regain control as he breathed through his clenched teeth.

"Hold still. We have to apply this to the burn. It's going to hurt like hell." He looked up at Aarne. "You OK?"

Aarne nodded and squeezed his eyes. The man smoothed a generous amount of the salve over his burn. Aarne cringed as it was applied, but it soothed the wound after the pain of being exposed to the air.

After a few minutes, Aarne felt relief. His heart rate slowed, and he relaxed his shoulders. He held his injured arm with his free hand, trying not to move it too much.

"Where did you get that stuff?" he asked.

"We were cleaning out one of the other buildings, and we found it. So of course we took it." The man smiled. "I didn't know we would need it so soon—or ever, actually."

"Your guardian angel must be looking out for you," Kalevi said. "That's a pretty bad burn, and you don't want it to get infected. It will probably leave a big scar."

For many days Aarne kept applying the salve to his wound, putting a thick coat over the red skin until eventually it began to heal. He wondered what he would have done had his shipmates not been there for him. It was always the way. When one of them was in need, another one came to the rescue.

He knew he was lucky. His accident could have been much worse, and if he couldn't work he would be of no use in camp. *And then,* he wondered, *what would happen to me?* He trembled at the thought.

For the next few weeks, the inmates worked in and around the evacuation camp. Early in the morning, after roll call, Aarne sat on a large wagon with rubber wheels, pulled by a horse, to be delivered to the bush, where he spent hours trying to cut down trees. Still exhausted from his sleepless night, he closed his eyes and slept in the back as the wagon jostled him and other inmates over the narrow, snow-covered bush roads. As the sun gained strength in the distance, he let its fingers caress his face even as the air chilled it like frosted glass. Sometimes he tucked his face between his bent knees, arms circling his legs until he created a little cocoon.

When they arrived at the clearing in the forest, Aarne woke to the sounds of men hustling out of the wagon and guards ordering them to hurry. Two by two, the men picked up long saws for cutting down the hardwood trees and making shorter logs. He grabbed one handle of the long device as another prisoner picked up the other end. Together the two sweated, pushing and pulling, pushing and pulling, back and forth until the saw's teeth chewed into the tree's trunk far enough that it would fall in the direction they planned or thereabout. It seemed to be an endless activity. Aarne had so little strength; his injured arm hurt with every movement, and he could barely pass the saw's teeth through the wood. His partner looked as exhausted as he did. As if by silent agreement, they kept moving in a show for the guards but expended as little energy as possible.

The logs were too heavy to carry, so they rolled them one by one up the pile, always ensuring the visible side of the pile looked to be at its full height for the benefit of the guards. The Polish farmer who owned the land looked kind and seemed to pity the concentration camp prisoners. But the guards—they expected the inmates to accomplish their work.

By the end of the day, Aarne marvelled at how little work they actually completed although they had been there for hours. He climbed into the V-shaped wagon, found a soft place on a pile of hay, and closed his eyes again, this time out of sheer exhaustion. His shoulders and arms ached, and the cold crept up from his feet, through his limbs, until every part of his body was frozen and stiff. He huddled in his clothes, jostled alongside the other men, who made themselves as comfortable as they could for the journey back to Tauenzin, where, he hoped, a meal of hot soup awaited them.

—ɯ—

One day during an afternoon off, Aarne was milling around the yard in a rare moment of free time when he realized the guards were looking to have some fun.

This can't be good, he thought. The victim was a friend—a French fellow he had met in Stutthof. While talking in a mixture of languages and gestures until they could mutually understand one another, he had learned the French man had blown up a part of a French railroad that was transporting German war materials; he had been arrested and sent by train to Stutthof. *Everyone has a story if only there is someone to listen*, Aarne thought.

"You, come here," the SS man said, pointing at the French man.

He did as he was told, taking off his hat in front of the guards, as was expected.

"Run." The guard pointed out towards the yard.

Confused and frightened, he started to jog. He was thin and bony, his shoes heavy on his feet. Aarne watched him reach the end of the yard and then turn around and return to the guards.

"Keep going. Run around the yard," the guard ordered. The other guards laughed and flicked their cigarette butts at the man as he passed by.

Confused, the French man ran around the camp, past the barracks and back again, creating a circular route. Each time he passed by the SS men, they kicked him with their jackboots. Aarne watched as his friend tired, his feet slipping on the snow below him.

"Faster. Faster," the guards shouted. The man tried to comply, but his legs looked as heavy as blocks of ice. Aarne noticed he could barely breathe in the cold air.

Aarne shook his head. "He can't go on much longer," he said to Kalevi.

"If he stops, they'll shoot him," Kalevi replied.

The SS stood with their arms crossed, laughing as the man's steps became less steady and his lines more jagged. He could barely raise his legs to take another step. He winced in pain with each vicious kick.

After several rounds of this, the Frenchman lay down on the ground and stopped moving. He took his last breath with his face cushioned against the snow.

"Move that body," a guard said, pointing at some nearby onlookers.

Three men lifted him from the snow, half dragging him to a pile of prisoners heaped by the barracks. The SS crew walked away, surely looking for some other amusement.

Aarne stood still. *If only I could have helped him*, he thought. But he knew there was nothing to be done.

—⚏—

The nights were endless. Aarne lay awake in his bunk, the air still around him. He pulled the thin sheet over his body, listening to the sounds of the dark. A few snores rose from his shipmates, the scurry of some small animal across the floor, the occasional creak in the wooden bunks as someone turned over. Aarne heard another sound. At first he wondered if it was an animal, but when he heard it again he decided to investigate.

Aarne crept from his bunk, tiptoeing over the sleeping bodies strewn across the floor, careful not to wake anyone. Cautiously he opened the door, holding his breath as it creaked. A rush of icy air filled his lungs and swatted his face. He closed the door behind him, hoping no one had noticed his movements.

Outside the barrack Aarne could see the monstrous mountain of the dead piled high, one on top of the other. It was a sight to which he could never get accustomed. He stopped to listen. He held his breath. Nothing moved. The pale light from the moon cast a strange glow on the snow, and the exaggerated shadows of the trees and barracks made it an eerie scene.

He heard it again. This time he knew it was the distinctive sound of a human moan. He inched along the wall, nearer to the pile of frozen bodies. Silence. He paused. Taking in a deep breath, he moved closer.

Aarne heard a whimper. This time he could see some slight movement from the stack of bodies. As his eyes adjusted to the semidarkness, he detected shifting in the sea of figures. With great effort a man was struggling to remove himself from the heap. He pulled himself up and hunched over on his hands and knees, the weight of the dead surrounding him. Aarne was amazed to see anyone alive and crept towards him, wondering how he could help.

Just as Aarne began moving, the sound of footsteps crunching the snow in his direction made him halt. He stepped back into the shadows, hoping he hadn't been noticed.

The guard approached the pile. The man looked up at the German with a gaping mouth and scared eyes. The guard stood over him for several seconds. Finally he shook his head.

"You were put there," the guard said, "and you stay there." The German took his rifle from his shoulder, repositioning it so the butt of the weapon faced the half-dead man. With a swift motion, the SS man struck the prisoner with one blow to the head. He dropped motionless on the ground, surrounded by those who had died before him.

Aarne winced as he witnessed the strike, feeling the shock reverberate from his toes. He waited a few more minutes, holding his breath, until he was sure the SS man had continued his rounds, and then he crept back into the barracks and into his bunk. The sounds of the night drifted in through the walls, but he heard no more moans from the dead.

—◊◊—

On a clear, cool afternoon, Aarne couldn't help but notice a female inmate leaning against a thin birch trunk, holding it with one hand for support. She was pale and gaunt. Even from a distance, her dark eyes sunk deep into her taut face. Aarne followed her eye line to the camp kitchen. The woman was watching something intently. She couldn't keep her eyes off it. Aarne moved closer to see what was happening that interested the girl so much.

A horse and buggy pulled up to the kitchen doors. Several inmates started unloading boxes of produce. Aarne glanced back at the girl, whose whole body seemed to lean towards the kitchen, her fingers gripping the tree trunk as if to keep her from falling over. The inmates stacked the contents of the buggy outside the doors: a load of fresh turnips, ready to be made into the tasteless soup.

Aarne looked back at the woman. Tall and thin like the branches of the birch tree, she could barely keep herself standing. He wondered what her plans were. Stealing from the camp kitchen would bring severe punishment. Should he warn her?

Before he could move, he saw a guard striding towards her. She was so intent on the activities at the kitchen that she did not even notice his heavy footsteps as he approached. She rested against the tree, still holding it with one arm. Aarne wondered if she might collapse.

Without saying a word to her, the guard approached. He took out his rifle.

Is he going to shoot her? Aarne wanted to yell or run, but she was too far away, and the guard would only turn on him.

The guard struck the trunk of the tree with the butt of his rifle. His blow was strong and decisive; the sound ricocheted against the barrack walls. Aarne watched as the woman slumped to the ground beneath the tree. There was no way she could survive the blow.

Aarne turned away.

—ᴡ—

One night Aarne awoke from a restless sleep to the sounds of the door slamming open and boots charging into the barracks. The others were immediately jostled from their light sleep as jackboots struck the wooden floors.

He peered through the dark room. The dark silhouette of a man hovered at the door. As his eyes adjusted, he could see the familiar SS uniform. In his hands the ominous figure held a rifle with a knife already attached to the end. What was he doing there in the middle of the night? Aarne tried to shake the cloudiness from his head.

The guard began yelling obscenities and looked menacingly around the room. The prisoners backed away, fearing his movement. Was he intoxicated? He was even more frenetic than most guards they had encountered.

Without hesitation the SS man struck at several people, stabbing his knife and swinging the rifle. He killed a few prisoners on the bottom bunks and injured several others as they tried to avoid him. Aarne pulled himself to the far corner of his bunk against the wall, pulling in his arms and legs against his chest, his body shaking.

The assault took only minutes, but it seemed like forever. The guards were notorious for being unpredictable, but Aarne had never seen one behave so erratically before. When the SS man stumbled out of the barrack, he left in his wake a shocked group of men, several injured and a few dead. Some had managed to flee from the room during the rampage, returning only when it seemed safe. With pounding hearts and shaking hands, they began helping the wounded and dealing with the dead. The camp continued to be more horrifying than Aarne could imagine.

—⁓—

Weeks passed. The squalid conditions deteriorated even as the winter weather was subdued by the promise of spring. By early March, more than five weeks after their arrival, Aarne heard that the front lines they had been fleeing were closing in on Tauenzin, and they would have to be evacuated again.

On March 9 Aarne was back on the road. As he left he realized that many of the prisoners, too sick or injured to march, were being left behind to die in the evacuation camp. Aarne counted his blessings. Of the more than one hundred Norwegians and Finns who had arrived at Tauenzin, all of them evacuated the camp, headed east towards Salino. He only wished his luck would not run out in the next part of this horrific journey.

GDAŃSK. Nad Mottawą

CHAPTER 13
Poland, March 1945

—⁓—

THE LONG WALK THROUGH Poland began again. Column eight trekked east, but the going was painfully slow. This time it seemed everyone was on the road as the Russians closed in. Aarne's group, greatly reduced since the first death march, was destined for Puck and Gydnia to the east, where, unbeknownst to Aarne, they would evacuate to Germany by sea. As the Red Army's tanks rolled in, civilians and prisoners fleeing the area were forced off the road to make way. He watched in horror as soldiers struck horses and caused civilian wagons, loaded with food, clothing, and other personal possessions, to tip over. The roads were filled with men, women, children, and the elderly trying to move away before the Russians arrived. The scene was one of chaos and desperation.

The warming sun had melted some of the snow, so boots and shoes kicked up both mud and slush. A group of civilians, pushing and pulling their wagons, made slow progress as they strained to move their heavy carts. It seemed an impossible task. Aarne watched as family groups struggled through the field, wondering what they would do when they reached the other side. Across the way yet another obstacle: high embankments circled the field. How would they get their wagons up the sides?

Aarne trudged behind his column, keeping a concerned eye on the civilians. Some pressed their whole bodies against their carts, digging their feet into the snow as they strained to move the wagons up the knoll. Others tried to pull the wagons, leaning forward with all of their weight. Every so often a wagon's wheel lodged in the thick sludge, forcing the family to dig it out of the mud. The going was slow—much slower than the sluggish movement of the prisoners.

"How are we going to get across this field?" Aarne asked. His boots were already wet and caked in mud.

Kalevi shook his head. "We can do it, but I don't know how those wagons will make it. That snow is melting into the ground so fast, it's just making a muddy mess."

All of a sudden, high above on the hills, Aarne could hear a low rumble. "What's that up there?" He squinted at the bright sun, trying to focus on the dark shapes as they emerged over the embankment.

"Tanks. Looks like Russian tanks."

They both stopped in their tracks, the mud sucking their boots into the ground.

Monstrous tanks gleamed, barrels facing into the field below. For a brief moment, the travellers, inmates, and civilians alike stood immobile. Children pointed and stared. Someone cried out. People abandoned their carts, scattering in every direction, frantically searching for shelter.

Aarne shrank to the ground. The tanks opened fire. He closed his eyes and wrapped his arms around his head. Machine gun fire vibrated across the valley. He felt the snow circle his wrists and the mud ooze between his fingertips. The smell of ancient dirt rose from the ground. Screams rang out. Children cried. He could hear a woman wailing. Civilians and prisoners fell, dotting the fields in red.

After a few minutes, the onslaught ceased as quickly as it had begun, and the tanks rumbled on, their massive bodies leaving behind a field littered with humans strewn in unnatural positions against the snow and mud. Aarne opened his eyes. The low groans of the tanks dissipated in the distance.

"Get up!" the guard commanded the prisoners. "Get into line."

Aarne pulled himself from the muddy ground, his limbs shaking.

"It's over now. Keep your lines moving," the guard ordered.

The column began marching again, pulling their feet through the thick sludge as they walked past the victims. Aarne glanced up at the ridge several times, but there was no sign of the monstrous beasts. When he reached the other side of the field, he paused again. The steep mound that had caused a problem for the wagons was now in front of him. He wasn't sure his legs would have the strength to climb the hill. The slippery snow and thick mud wouldn't help him either.

The guards stood aside, yelling at the prisoners. "Let's go. Faster."

Aarne tried to scurry up the hill as quickly as he could, but his boots were soon covered in a thick blanket of muck that made his feet heavy. He landed on his knees and scrambled with his hands before reaching the top. Behind him lay a mass of dead and dying scattered across the open field. He could not look back.

—⁓—

As the light dimmed, Aarne looked forward to the next stopping place, a chance to dry off perhaps and rest his body for a few hours. He expected the sleeping conditions to be pitiable, but anything was better than the constant trudging.

In the distance he spied a large farmhouse, a wooden barn, and a shed surrounded by fields and bordered by a forest. Behind the structures the sun, low on the horizon, painted a canvas of yellow, pink, and purple. Long shadows danced on the snow. It was a peaceful scene, even picturesque except that in minutes prisoners would overrun it looking for sleeping places.

There was no sign of the inhabitants. Like so many others, they must have abandoned their home. Soon the best spots were claimed in the large barn, away from the rising wind and blowing snow. Aarne wrapped his arms around his torso, pulling his collar around his ears as he searched inside for a small space to call his own for the night, but he could find nowhere to lie down. Whenever he found a suitable space, someone glared at him or told him to move on, the spot was taken.

He followed a few of the other unlucky ones to a large shed behind the barn. It was little more than a wooden lean-to with a roof and three walls but no fourth wall or door. *It will do*, he thought. At least the walls would cut the wind and keep off most of the snow. A strong whiff of old farming equipment and rotting hay greeted him as he nestled into a corner. Old hay was strewn on the wooden planks, providing some comfort from the hard floor.

This wasn't the first time he slept in a lean-to. He rested his head against a wall, wrapping his arms around his knees to stay warm. Quiet conversations from the other corner, a few moans from an old man, and the restless movement of uncomfortable sleepers became background noise as he settled in for a long night, hoping he would be able to sleep with the wind howling through the open structure, sending with it flecks of blowing snow.

A dark sky dotted with twinkling stars surrounded the farm. A few hours into a restless sleep, Aarne awoke to a shockwave shattering through his body. In the nearby barn, hand grenades exploded. Screams of terror rang through the night air. Dazzling lights illuminated the windows. The barn was burning.

Rat-a-tat-tat. Rat-a-tat-tat. Within seconds the nearby eruptions shocked the other prisoners awake, leaving them momentarily dazed. Screams and gunfire echoed against the buildings. The night sky was set alight from below in an inferno of reds and yellows. Ghastly shadows danced and licked at walls. Aarne stared in terror. An acrid taste and grey smoke overpowered his senses.

With the outbuilding ablaze, chaos erupted. Prisoners and German soldiers alike spread in every direction.

The Russians had arrived.

The dark outline of three ominous figures stood in front of the lean-to. Aarne's eyes widened. He sat frozen in a dark corner, barely able to breathe for fear. The silhouettes stood motionless, feet planted firmly, armed with machine guns. A few words in Russian followed by rapid fire into the dark shed, back and forth, left and right. Machine guns rat-a-tat-tatted. Prisoners screamed. Bodies thudded as they hit the floor.

Aarne scuttled out of the shed. He ran past the burning barn and across the field, trying to stay in the shadows of the trees that dotted their way towards the forest. When he had made it some distance from the buildings, he ducked into some low-lying bushes. His body shook from shock and cold as he watched the barn blazing against the sky.

What was happening? He tried to slow his breath, calm his racing heart, and sort out the details. That they were Russians was certain. But shouldn't they be trying to liberate the prisoners, not massacre them? In the distance machine gun fire continued to reverberate intermittently. Russian voices shouted commands. Several soldiers ran from barn to house and shed. He wasn't sure what to do, so he waited, trembling, alone and in the dark.

From his hiding place, Aarne heard a German swearing and mumbling to himself as he struggled to dislodge the wheel of a wagon from its muddy grip. The uniformed man was clearly one of the SS guards, trying to escape the Russians. Aarne didn't wait to see the end result. Staying low to the ground and in the shadow of the bushes, he snuck past the preoccupied guard.

The forest enveloped him as he moved stealthily through the trees. When he believed he was safely past the guard, he paused. For a moment he held his breath. If someone were following, surely he would hear footsteps in the undergrowth. Nothing. He let out a silent sigh and continued on, ducking low and creeping from tree to tree.

As soon as he was out of earshot, Aarne ran through the woods in the darkness, stumbling over fallen tree trunks, not knowing where he was going or how he had managed to escape the bloodbath. His heart continued to pound against his chest as he struggled to breathe air into his belaboured lungs. He travelled through the undergrowth until his legs finally gave way. Hiding himself under some bushes, he hoped he would awaken to see daylight again.

—⟪—

Early the next morning, as the sun peered through the canopy of interlaced branches, Aarne awoke, remembering what had happened in the pandemonium of the previous night. He imagined he could still hear the blazing of the barn, the incessant chatter of machine guns, and the panicked screams of the prisoners.

Before sitting up he looked around, trying to control his quickening breath, the steam from his exhalations evaporating like smoke from a chimney into the crisp air. The dawn greeted him with the swishing of pine needles, the chirping of birds, and the shushing of the breeze. He listened to the sounds of the forest floor. No gunshots, no bombs, no yelling guards, no moaning prisoners. For the first time in many months, he was utterly alone. The morning was filled with pleasant sounds.

Aarne brushed the snow from his clothes, listening for the noise of human movement. The only sounds were the hums of nature waking in the early morning—sounds that had been there long before he had arrived and would continue long after he passed.

This was his chance to get away from the Germans and escape the Russians. This was his chance for freedom. He needed to get as much distance between himself and the barn as possible, but which direction was the safest?

Aarne travelled through the bush and the outskirts of the forest. As the morning hours passed, the sun began to warm the air. The faint light between the tree branches suggested an open area in the distance. Perhaps it was a clearing. Maybe a road. He walked towards the light, ever vigilant for the signs or sounds of movement. Eventually he came to the edge of the forest, to a long country road curving into the distance. It seemed quiet. He kept trekking but stayed near the lane, hoping it would lead somewhere. Anywhere. Once in a while, he felt relief. If he closed his eyes, he could imagine he was in a distant northern park, the river humming beside him, a white footbridge waiting to lead him safely home. But mostly he felt anxious.

The sun's rays played between the branches, warming him as he put several kilometres between himself and the farm. The afternoon wore on. For now, he felt, it was safest to keep off the roads. Sometimes he rested, eating from patches of clean snow circling the tree trunks.

As the sun dipped back down to the horizon, the shadows lengthened around him. It brought a chill that Aarne could not shake. His desire for freedom, so acute in the morning, had waxed and waned; he was near collapse. It was not yet dark, but he could travel no farther, so he crawled under a nearby bush, waiting for the cold to take him like one of the many white statues he had passed on the death march. Perhaps a

Nazi or a Russian soldier would find and shoot him. How the end would come, he did not know. But he could go on no longer. His last sliver of hope diminished behind a black cloud.

—⁓—

The next morning he awoke to find himself under the tangled branches of a bush, wondering where he was. His head was muddled and filled with questions. *Which way should I go? What should I do? Towards the Russians? Towards the Germans?* None of these options seemed appealing, but his desire to continue moving, to live, had returned with the first glimmer of morning light.

Stiff and sore, he pulled himself to his feet. His body ached, and he was hungry as he made his way close to the road. He looked down one side as far as he could. No signs of horses or trucks. He scanned the forest across the road and then turned his gaze to the other direction. To his surprise two men were sitting at the side of the road, their jackets pulled up around their ears, knees tucked into their chins. *Were they Germans, Russians, or civilians?* he wondered. Perhaps they were fellow escapees. He couldn't even be sure if they were alive; they sat so still, like frozen figures carved in the landscape. Aarne considered his options. If he got up, they might run off, or they might attack. He inched himself closer and closer, trying to get a better look.

As he got nearer, Aarne recognized the men. The taller of the two wore a faded Italian army uniform like those issued to the Norwegian policemen at Stutthof. He knew this man, Erik, from the barrack. The other man, Lars, was shorter and wore worn-out civilian clothes. They were Norwegian policemen. Both were thin and pale, their clothes draped loosely around their lean limbs. He smiled and breathed a sigh of relief.

"Psst. Psst," Aarne whispered, trying to get their attention without scaring them away.

Lars looked up, his eyes widening as he recognized Aarne from the camp. He nudged his dozing friend.

"Erik, wake up. Look who we have here."

Erik turned his droopy eyes towards Aarne. "What are you doing here?" His eyes widened. "How did you get out of that mess?"

Aarne told them about his travels but wasn't really sure how he had managed to escape the machine gun fire in the shed. It was all a blur. The Norwegians shared a similar story, feeling lucky they had survived. They too had escaped the massacre but couldn't really say exactly how they had gotten away from the chaos. They had hidden in the woods nearby until it seemed safe enough to travel.

"I thought you were a German or Russian when I first saw you," Erik said. "You frightened the hell out of me."

"I wasn't sure about you two either," Aarne replied. "The Italian suit gave it away." He grinned. It felt good to be talking to them. He would no longer need to be alone and afraid.

—⁂—

For many days the three escapees travelled together, walking off the main highway and bush roads, through towns and villages, trying to stay hidden from prying eyes. They saw many others along the road, mainly civilians, some Ukrainians and Jews, but didn't see any other Scandinavian prisoners from their group.

"It's a good thing we don't have the striped prisoner clothes," Aarne remarked one day. "We blend in better with the population this way. Even that old Italian uniform looks more likely than the camp uniform."

Once again he was thankful for his German jackboots. Without them he never could have survived the winter in the camp, let alone the death march or his current journey.

"You look like you need a bath, Aarne," Lars remarked. He looked down at his own dishevelled clothes and smelled the armpit of his jacket.

"I guess we all do." He laughed. "Not very likely, I suppose. But we really do need to find food. I'm not sure how much longer I can go on without it."

Aarne agreed. Finding food was always their first priority.

After several kilometres of walking, Erik noticed some movement across a field. A group of Polish labourers was entering an old school building.

"Hey, look over there. I bet those men have some food," he said.

"But what if it's a prison camp, like Stutthof?" Aarne worried about the look of the place. The area was surrounded by a fence, but the labourers did not look like the prisoners of Stutthof, and the guards were not Nazis. There were no watchtowers.

"I think they're just workers," Lars replied. "And look. Food."

Aarne's stomach grumbled. He watched as the labourers returned from the building with bowls of steaming soup. Aarne imagined he could smell the broth from where he was hidden.

"Let's go." Erik looked at Aarne and Lars. They nodded in agreement. "Just try to blend in, like we're with them."

They lined up behind a group beyond the fence outside the school. Aarne tried to keep his head down as he waited in the food line. A worker ladled the fragrant soup until it filled his bowl. The Scandinavians cupped their warm bowls, enjoying the steam rising to their nostrils, and drank their meal with fervour. Afterward they casually walked around the yard for a while, trying to blend in.

"What do you think? Should we stay here for the night?" Aarne asked as the workers began to disperse to their sleeping quarters.

"It would be nice to be warm and dry for once," Lars said.

"I don't see why not. They gave us soup, didn't they?" The men smiled.

Aarne and his friends looked in each room. All of the lodgings were full; people were lying on the floors, crammed tightly together. Eventually they found a room that had some space. Aarne tried to walk in with confidence and lie on the floor beside the strangers. A few fellows looked at him suspiciously but didn't say a word. He felt safe and secure for the first time in ages. He slept.

The next morning Aarne woke to the movement and rumblings of the others. Again he joined Erik and Lars as they lined up to enjoy the plain breakfast of tea and hot soup. Once the labourers finished their morning rations, they began forming work groups.

"Let's follow them to the gate, then we can get going," Aarne suggested.

The three pretended to be part of the crowd, but as the labourers continued down the road, they ducked into the woods. If anyone noticed that they left the line, none said anything. They hid in the bush until the workers passed.

The three wandered near the road, hoping to find more food or a place to hide. Aarne was startled by the sound of gunfire nearby.

"Russians everywhere, I think," he said. "They sound really close."

"We're not out of danger yet," Erik replied. "Keep your eyes open."

As the men walked, they noticed a man riding by with three horses at his side. Without warning a grenade suddenly exploded in the street, blasting the ground below the horses' feet. Aarne was stunned. Shrieks filled the air as blood flowed from the horses' necks. Only one horse remained standing, blood pouring from its neck where shrapnel had hit it. The whites of its eyes showed its fear as its legs gave out, and it collapsed on the street with a crash.

Aarne turned his eyes away from the sight. He had seen every kind of death imaginable; he didn't need to see any more. Not even these gentle creatures could escape the constant rapping of death at the door.

Finding food and shelter continued to be a priority for the three men. One day, as they were travelling, Aarne saw a little, wooden house on the side of the road. It sat neatly at the edge of a field, the forest looming behind it. They observed it for a long time, waiting to see any signs of life. No one came in or out of the house. They could see no shadows behind the windows.

"Maybe it's empty," Aarne said.

"Maybe they're just hiding." Lars looked intently at the darkened house. "We shouldn't take any chances."

They watched awhile longer. The sun made steady progress across the clear sky. Aarne could feel the void in his stomach grow and his insides grumble.

"Let's go. There's only one way to find out." Erik stood up. Aarne and Lars followed suit. The three crossed the street with long steps.

Aarne approached the door. He stopped, looking at the others. In silence they both nodded. He grabbed the doorknob, turned it slowly, and pushed the door open, cringing as the hinges creaked. As quietly as he could, he entered the ancient building.

The house appeared abandoned. Aarne glanced at the worn furniture. Dusty family photographs lined a shelf. Dishes lingered where the owners had left them. Something spoiled secreted a putrid smell. *No signs of anyone, at least not recently*, he thought.

Feeling more confident, Aarne stepped into the kitchen, eager to find some scraps of food, hopeful that the inhabitants of the house hadn't taken everything with them. Suddenly he stopped in his tracks. Sitting at the round kitchen table, an old man with wrinkles around his deep-set eyes glared up at him. Aarne didn't move. He looked down at the man's bony fingers clutched around a shoemaker's iron hammer. It shook in his hands.

"I don't want any trouble," Aarne said, holding up his open hands to show the old man he was unarmed.

"It's OK, now." Erik spoke in soothing tones as he tiptoed into the room. "We don't want to hurt you. We're just looking for some food." He motioned the action of eating with three fingers to his mouth and pretended to chew.

The shoemaker, thin and wiry, looked from one man to the other. He was clearly outnumbered despite the weakened state of the intruders. Surrounded by the tools of his trade, the old man began yelling in Polish. They couldn't understand his words, but his message was clear.

"Don't worry, don't worry." Lars tried to calm the man, knowing the shoemaker wouldn't understand his language. He looked at his friends. "I think he wants us out of his kitchen."

The frail Polish man continued to yell, swinging his hammer as though to hit the Scandinavians. Aarne jumped as the hammer hit the table with a bang. He stepped back, his hands still in the air.

"It's OK. We're going," Erik said. Before he turned to leave, his hand shot out to grab a loaf of bread from the table, dodging the old man's hammer. Then he ran out the door.

Aarne and Lars followed suit. The Polish shoemaker was so frail and feeble, the three of them could easily have taken him, but they had no desire to do him any harm. Aarne felt sorry for the old man. How could he possibly survive on his own in that house until the end of the war? He didn't blame the Polish shoemaker for not assisting them. If the shoemaker helped them, he would be placing himself in grave danger if the Nazis were to find out. Aarne had no interest in creating more problems for the old fellow. His only concern was getting a bit of the bread.

Eventually the escapees made it to Danzig, only thirty or so kilometres away from the concentration camp, and the same harbour where the Germans had arrested Aarne.

"Do you know your way around, Aarne?" Lars asked.

"I've been here many times with the crew, but it doesn't look familiar anymore." He surveyed the devastation. It looked difficult to navigate. "The buildings are unrecognizable. I can't even tell where the streets begin and end. There was a Swedish sailors' church somewhere in Danzig.

Maybe if we go there, they can give us some food and a place to sleep. They might even help us get to Sweden and then home." Aarne's heart lightened.

The three travelled down several badly bombed streets, stumbled over rubble, and searched the remains of buildings, looking for anything familiar or edible. It was not the same town Aarne remembered. Partial walls of jagged brick suggested what a building might once have looked like. They walked through the destruction but couldn't find the church or anyone who could help them.

"I'm sorry. I have no idea which way we should go. That church could be anywhere. Maybe it doesn't even exist anymore." Aarne's face darkened. The dream of the sailors' church died as dark shadows crept through the streets. "Let's find somewhere to sleep in one of these buildings before it gets too dark to see."

They entered a dusty, old abandoned building. It was drafty but quiet. They inspected all of the rooms, hoping to find some food, but everything had been taken or destroyed.

The next morning Erik suggested a plan. "Listen, maybe I can find that church on my own. Don't worry. I'll come back for you," he said. "I think my clothes are in better shape than yours. I might have more success talking to the locals."

Aarne and Lars agreed. They stayed in the dingy building, noting the desolation the darkness had covered the previous night. *It's unlikely anyone is left in Danzig*, Aarne thought.

A few hours later, his friend came back disappointed. He couldn't find the church, and he hadn't seen anyone who would help. Nothing was as it had been.

They managed to scrounge for some food, getting stronger as they ate and rested. A few days after their arrival, they started to relax. Perhaps they felt a little too brave. They began walking through town without trying to hide. They hadn't seen any Nazi or Russian soldiers for days.

—ᴧᴧ—

One morning they saw an old Polish couple walking down the cobble-stone streets. The pair eyed them suspiciously, clinging to one another's arms.

"Do you have any food?" Lars asked. Again he pretended to eat. The Polish couple shook their heads and toddled off, arm in arm through the rubble, dust rising behind them. Lars looked up at Erik, who shrugged his shoulders. "We'll try somewhere else."

The men continued to search every abandoned building. Eventually, as they scavenged room by room, they met some more locals.

"Do you have anything for us to eat?" Aarne asked, trying not to scare them off. He moved towards them with caution.

They gave him some ration cards, indicating they were for food. Aarne nodded and smiled, thanking them again and again.

"Where are we going to use those? They're useless if there aren't any stores." Erik complained. "We need bread. We need soup, not some use-less ration cards." The frustration emanated from his body.

Aarne sighed, pocketing the cards just in case. The men continued to search the houses and stores, finding others had looted there before them. Only occasionally could they find some scrap of almost edible food.

—ᴧᴧ—

After several days in Danzig, their search for food led them to the main railroad station. There seemed to be some activity. Where there were people, there might be food, Aarne rationalized.

Aarne looked at the other two, his eyes twinkling as the smell of cof-fee and cooking streamed out of the building. A slight smile formed on his lips. To their surprise, the railroad coffee shop was still operating. A few people sat at the scattered tables, drinking coffee and eating bread or pastries.

Aarne envied the people who were probably waiting for a train to take them away from this place. He had nothing. No food. No money. No hope.

He and the others assessed the situation from a distance. There was definitely food to be had, but how to get it? The scent of coffee and aromas of cooking drifting in from a kitchen made Aarne's mouth water.

Finally Erik could wait no longer. Aarne watched as he moved swiftly towards one of the tables. With a hasty hand he grabbed some food from a plate and then turned to flee. Before he could run out of the station, a Nazi soldier's imposing body blocked him. He tried to dodge the soldier, but it was no use. Another soldier appeared in the other direction. He was trapped.

Aarne watched in astonishment as the soldier seized Erik. From seemingly nowhere other soldiers appeared and rushed towards Aarne and Lars, seizing both of them before they were able to bolt. For the second time, all three escapees were arrested.

"What'll happen now?" Aarne asked as he sat on the concrete floor of his temporary jail cell in the train station.

"Do you think they will kill us?" Lars hung his head.

"Who knows what they'll do. Maybe we'll be sent back to Stutthof or some other camp."

"If they find out we are escaped prisoners, they'll probably shoot us," Erik said. "Escapees don't get a second chance."

Aarne shuddered. Darkness crept into the small room, but no one came to move them out. Eventually Aarne rested his head on the floor, unable to close his eyes. He watched the shadows on the wall twisting and turning as if in a horrific dream. He waited.

—∞—

The next day the three escapees were placed on a railway car bound for Stutthof, a journey that was all too familiar to Aarne. He couldn't help but worry about his fate. Escaped prisoners from Stutthof were usually executed.

When they arrived the tall, wooden death gate swung open for them. Aarne took this opportunity to enter the camp's yard, already teeming with prisoners, before the soldiers could stop him. He mixed with a group, trying to blend in so the guards wouldn't question or identify him. Within seconds he and his Norwegian friends had disappeared into the prison population, returning to numbers instead of names, men with no identities. This time it worked in their favour.

"Aarne, it's you. I can't believe you're alive. We believed you were shot in the barn," Kalevi looked surprised and relieved. "What happened?"

Aarne explained how he had managed to escape the massacre, how he had found the Norwegians, and all of their adventures leading to their rearrest at the Danzig railroad station.

Aarne's Finnish friends had only arrived in Stutthof a few days earlier.

"After the Russians bombed the barn, many of the prisoners had tried to run away, but the Germans rounded them up. Those who survived the massacre were marched to Danzig and then housed in another camp for several days before being sent here," Kalevi said. "Every day more prisoners are returning, but the camp is still much smaller than when we left. That's why we're all in the old camp. No reason to be in Sonderlager anymore with so much space for us here."

Aarne nodded. "Did everyone from our ship make it?" Aarne asked, worried about the response.

"So far I think we're all OK," Kalevi said.

Aarne felt relief. He was thankful to be with his Finnish shipmates again and even more grateful to be alive. He had witnessed hundreds die along the evacuation route, in the Tauenzin camp, and at the hands of the Russians. He was safely returned to the camp, at least for now.

CHAPTER 14

Return to Stutthof, April 1945

—꿈—

AARNE LOOKED OUT THE window, the sick feeling in his stomach returning. His new barrack, at the far end of the block in the old camp, was much like his previous hut. His view was not. It was still early morning, and the sun was only beginning to peek through the pine trees, but he took no notice of the dense forest hugging the eastern edge of the camp beyond the barbed wires. Instead he gaped at the less pleasant scene to the left, twisting a piece of paper between his thumb and forefinger as he fell deep into thought.

"Aarne," Kalevi said. "Can you give me a hand?"

"Have you even looked at this?" He glanced back at his friend.

"The kapos could be here at any minute for an inspection. You'd better get your bunk in order." Kalevi tried to tuck the grey, tattered blanket into the far corner of the top bed.

Aarne was drawn back to the ghastly view of the crematory, with its three oil-fuelled ovens and eighteen-metre-tall chimney. Across from it stood the small, red brick gas chamber with its concrete floor and metal doors. He remembered being marched to have his clothes disinfected in that very gas chamber and shuddered when he learned that prisoners had been exterminated there using Zyklon B pellets. It was a small chamber, but large enough to murder many people at one time. He wondered how many had lost their lives in that dark space.

Prisoners perished. That was the reality. In November and January, a typhus epidemic caused many deaths, but others died because they were simply too weak, malnourished, and overworked. Others were beaten or publically executed. Every morning, as he went about his daily routine, Aarne watched the cart stopping at the doors of each of the barracks, collecting corpses. A contingent of prisoners carried out the bodies, unceremoniously throwing them on the others in the wooden cart. Each stop made their load heavier. He looked at their faces, the men whose job it was to deal with the dead. Their bodies drooped, their eyes expressed no emotion, and they rarely spoke. It was a heavy burden indeed.

"Aarne, come away from there," Kalevi said, the concern for his friend evident in his voice.

The stench was unbearable. The horrible mixture of rotting flesh and burning bodies was inescapable. It seemed that no matter when he looked out the window, the crematory's chimney, its smoke spiralling up into a black cloud, was in constant use. Aarne's eyes travelled from the dark cloud, down the chimney to the base of the building. A heap of emaciated bodies, like broken matchsticks, piled several high, waited to be disposed of in the ovens. Aarne cringed at the thin arms and legs jutting out at odd angles and the gaunt faces, with lifeless eyes and gaping mouths. It seemed the Germans could not keep up with the demands of the dead. Other prisoners reported black smoke rising through the trees both day and night from a clearing in the forest north of the new camp. The stink of burning flesh now surrounded him.

Aarne pulled himself away from the window, away from the grim scene that both saddened and sickened him. He would never be able to remove that grisly sight from his memory. He would never be able to forget the stench.

"I just don't understand," Aarne replied. "How can anyone treat his fellow human beings like this? Like animals?" His shoulders sagged as he sat on his low bunk.

"Do you want me to help you with your blanket?" Kalevi asked.

"Some of the stories are so incredible, I don't know what to believe. You know, I heard some rumours about a doctor from Danzig," one of the sailors said as he leaned across his bunk to make his bed. "They say he's collecting the bodies of the Jews to make soap from their fat."

Aarne looked up, his nose crinkled in disgust. "That's just horrible. How could anyone even think about doing that? And who would use it anyway? Besides, I can't imagine they would have any fat left on them after being here. They're so thin, you can practically see their bones." Several times before, he had wondered at the frailty of the Jewish prisoners in the new camp. Their conditions seemed even worse than his, if that were possible.

"I know. It's hard to believe. Nothing makes sense here." The sailor turned to tidy his bunk.

Aarne stood up and took the edge of his own blanket. Kalevi helped with the other side. As they stretched it over the bunk and tucked it tightly at the edges, the ghastly images still burned in Aarne's mind.

—ⅲ—

The winter deep freeze had warmed to a spring thaw. Aarne was on trench digging duty at the north end of the camp, with one of the most brutal kommandos. Outside work meant difficult physical labour and exposure to the unpredictable elements.

With roll call and rations done for the morning, Aarne grabbed a shovel from the pile and joined his kommando for the march to the field. By then new buds on the trees and the beginnings of grass in the fields were replacing the snow. He took his place in a long line, digging the dark dirt, creating a deep trench in preparation for the defence against the advancing Red Army. Some of the prisoners shovelled into the hillside, creating a secret place for the Germans to hide their military equipment.

As he swung his shovel, Aarne listened to the whirr of Russian airplanes, gradually increasing to a blare as they soared over Stutthof throughout the day. The intermittent sounds of strafing and explosives kept him on high alert. Occasionally the planes seemed to come close to the men in the trenches. When they did he squinted into the sky, gripped the shovel in his hands, and made ready to dodge away or jump into the trench. But it didn't seem that the aircraft were interested in attacking the camp. *Were they aware that it housed prisoners?* Aarne wondered. The German army stationed nearby, on the other hand, was continually bombed. He could hear the bursts of explosions and sometimes feel the reverberations travel through his shovel into his hands.

The afternoon was heating up. Sweat drenched his back. Occasionally he stopped to wipe the sweat from dripping into his eyes. Without warning he heard the fast approach of an airplane. This time it was different. He glanced up to see the shiny underbelly gleaming in the sunlight. It was coming their way.

"Take shelter," he heard in German. Aarne dove down into the dirt, covering his head with his hands and holding his breath, hoping the trenches were not the target. Within seconds he heard the explosion. It came from the direction of the camp.

"Get up and start digging." The guard threatened. "Get up, you lazy pigs. Get to work."

Aarne looked up from the bottom of the trench. Already the guards were positioned above them, yelling orders and brandishing weapons, delivering severe blows to those who didn't comply in good speed. He scrambled to his legs, picked up his shovel, and continued his relentless digging. His hands shook as he gripped the shovel. His shoulders ached, and the dirt from the trench stuck to his sweaty clothes. Glancing up to the clear sky, he wondered if another plane was on its way.

When Aarne returned from his work duty, a small group of the sailors had gathered in the clearing in front of the barracks, drawn and weary expressions on many of the men's faces. Perhaps they had news. He stopped at the edge of the group to listen.

"You heard that an explosion hit the camp?" one of the sailors said.

"I saw the plane overhead. It sounded so close that we ran for cover. We thought it might have landed somewhere inside the camp this time," another said.

"It did. It struck the kitchen," the sailor replied. "Bread and potatoes flew in all directions, like manna from heaven, raining down on the prisoners. You wouldn't believe the sight. The people scattered in every direction, like ants seeking crumbs, gathering whatever food they could find." The sailor paused. "But then the guards noticed what was happening. They stood in their watchtowers and opened fire. They killed anyone who was trying to pick up the food." He stopped, unable to continue.

Aarne looked at him in disbelief.

"But that's not all. Several people who were in the kitchen when it was bombed were killed. We lost one of the women from a Finnish ship." The sailor looked at the floor.

Aarne felt his stomach drop. So far the Finnish sailors and crew members had managed to survive life in Stutthof. This bombing seemed so senseless. Why would the Russians target a camp filled with prisoners? He didn't know what to think. Clearly the others didn't either as they stood in silence.

—◊—

Day after day Aarne worked in the trenches. By early April Commandant Hoppe had departed from the camp along with many of the SS crew, leaving SS Hauptsturmführer Paul Ehle in charge of camp proceedings. Over time discipline in the camp decreased, and the guards even conducted roll call with less precision than before. The inmates could no longer rely on the camp kitchen for regular rations.

One day Aarne overheard some inmates talking about how the guards had found some stray horses and led them into camp. They probably belonged to the German civilians or military personnel who were in the process of evacuating the area, leaving the creatures behind to wander aimlessly.

As Aarne worked, he recalled the horses near his childhood house in the Kuusiluoto neighbourhood. On a summer evening the neighbours left the heat of their homes to relax under the birch trees, listening to the sounds of water lapping against the shore as a cool breeze rustled the leaves and the sun set on the horizon. The parents drank coffee and gossiped together, sharing the day's news as the children played in a field nearby. The fenced field housed beautiful horses and served as a perfect place for Aarne and his friends—Olli, a very tall young man nicknamed Viitako Kuningas, or Jungle King, by Aarne's father; and the twins, nicknamed Niku and Naku after the twins in Donald Duck—to play cowboys. The memory made Aarne smile. Just as quickly sadness overcame him.

After trench duty he returned to his barrack. The men were talking excitedly.

"What's going on?" he asked.

"A horse. A few men managed to catch one of those horses," Kalevi replied.

"They tied barbed wire around its massive neck, pulling it tight until the wire sliced through its solid flesh. Then they waited as it bled to death."

"That's not all. They caught a second horse and led it into a barrack, where it went crazy with fear. I guess the space was too small for the poor thing. It started kicking and bolting, even turning over the table with great force. I'm not sure who was more scared, the horse or the prisoners. Eventually they managed to calm it down before it destroyed the whole hut or hurt one of them."

"What happened to it?" Aarne asked.

"What do you think happened?" The man grinned at him. "They ate it. They skewered pieces and seared it over a fire. Only problem was, some of them just couldn't wait for the meat to be cooked. They drank the warm blood and ate the horse meat raw. They got sick as anything."

Aarne didn't respond. It was hard to imagine killing the animal, but meat was meat, and any opportunity to eat might save lives.

A few days later, Aarne and the crew working in the trenches noticed one of the horses grazing on a small patch of fresh grass.

"What do you think, boys? Should we try to get it?" The message went down the line. It was near the end of the workday, and the guards were preoccupied.

It took some time, but they eventually coaxed the large creature closer. As with the other horses, they used a wire around this one's neck, pulling it tight until it sliced the flesh and blood began to pour to the ground. It didn't take long before the animal dropped with a thud. The inmates cut it into many smaller pieces and distributed the meat among the workers.

When Aarne took his piece, he was grateful for the food, but he frowned at the size. It was from the lower part of the leg and had very little flesh. He resisted the urge to take a bite as he carried his prize back to the camp, remembering how sick some of the prisoners had been when they ate the uncooked meat. Some, he learned, had even died. Although he was starving, he put the leg into a pot of boiling water. The fat from the horse's leg floated thickly to the top. He watched the water bubbling, his mouth watering with anticipation. He was right. There was not much meat on the leg, but he ate what little flesh there was, picking it off of the bones, thankful to have even this much.

—⟋⟍—

Aarne dug his shovel into the soil, pulling the dirt up and tossing it aside. By then, seven months into captivity, the torment of what could loosely be called living had taken its toll. He drove his shovel into the dirt a second time. Suddenly he was overcome. The physical exhaustion and mental fatigue drained him of energy. He could not imagine another moment in this hell.

I have to get out of here, he thought. *Now.*

His eyes on the guards, Aarne made tentative steps towards the bushes at the perimeter of the field. He was afraid to make any sudden movement. Luckily the guards were a fair distance from his area of the trench, and their attention seemed to be elsewhere. He lowered the shovel and hid it in some bushes. His feet searched the ground behind him. Clutching the sides of his pants, he crouched down as if to relieve himself in the bush, just in case a guard happened to look in his direction.

His breathing slowed until it almost stopped; his heart pounded, and his hands trembled. With one cautious movement after another, he slunk to the ground until, snakelike, he slid backwards into the grass. Crawling his way from bush to bush, he kept low, hoping to blend with his terrain. Sometimes he paused to peer up at the prisoners and glance at the guards, who were unaware that their numbers had decreased by one. Behind him the denser bushes of the forest beckoned. It took him several anxious minutes before he entered its protective coverage. Finally he breathed again.

Danzig Bay was his only hope. He knew to head north until he hit the Baltic coast. Somehow, if he could only get to the sea...

"Over there...there," a German voice said, followed by rapid footsteps crunching leaves and snapping branches. He could see two sets of shiny jackboots partially obstructed by the bushes. He followed the boots up, past the grey trousers and jackets to the strong-jawed men with blue eyes. Two Nazis, their guns aimed and ready, pointed to the ground.

Aarne's muscles froze. He caught his breath.

Bang. One of the soldiers took a shot. Aarne pressed his face against the dirt.

"You missed it. It's over there." Aarne peered up but tried to keep his head down. The two men were laughing now and running after something in the bushes. A rabbit. He could hear its scampering and just make out its furry form before it bounded through the underbrush.

Aarne released the tension in his body and let out a long and steady stream of breath. The soldiers, following their prey, headed in one direction, and Aarne, like the rabbit hiding in the brush, went the other.

For some distance he travelled in the direction of the coast, stopping occasionally to listen to the sounds of the woods, worried about any human contact. He believed the coast was only a few kilometres away, but his pace was slow. *Better to be cautious*, he thought. *Stay focused.*

Before he reached the shore, the beckoning sounds of crashing waves and the sweet smell of sea salt filled the air. He was getting close. Several metres of shoreline encircled the bay, defined by great mounds of sand and waving dune grass. Beyond the shore pine and fir trees created shade and privacy for the escaped prisoner.

Aarne drank in the sight. For a long time, he lay in the undergrowth near the strand, hidden from view, wondering at the beauty of the sea that had long since given him up to his captors but promised to deliver him home one day. In the distance, past the white-tipped waves of the bay, the cobalt sea merged with the endless sky. It was a stunning sight. Birds flew freely above him, calling to one another over the sounds of the sea. Waves lapped at the shoreline while a breeze rustled the needles of the pine trees.

Aarne imagined sailing away into the horizon. For a moment, on this beach, he felt free from imprisonment, torture, hunger, forced labour, and nightmares. He imagined his life as it had been and as it could be again.

Aarne's brief dream was shattered with the sound of footsteps and German voices. He ducked his head and listened intently. Somewhere above him, he could just make out the shape of a wooden structure in the trees. A Nazi lookout.

I can't stay here, he thought. *They'll find me.* He dropped his body lower, onto his belly, and crept from his hiding place as noiselessly as he could. One last glance at the Baltic, and he was away.

There was nowhere for him to go, no way to hide from the guards, no means to escape this land even by his beloved sea. Deflated, he retraced his steps from the fine sand beach, through the forest, to the open crop fields. Within hours he was back in the field behind the camp, where he had been digging trenches. By then it was dark, and the prisoners had already returned to the barracks. His body sank like mortar to the ground, and he slept fitfully until dawn.

With the first light of morning, Aarne woke, disorientated to find he was alone in the open field. He waited for his prison mates to return to the trenches, grabbed the shovel hidden in the grass, and joined the surprised Finns, unnoticed by the soldiers.

"What happened to you?" Someone whispered to Aarne as he took his place on the trench line. He told them briefly, promising to give them more details later when they were out of the guard's earshot.

Later that day, while eating rations on the ground near the trenches, Aarne shared the story of his daring escape.

"You were so lucky, Aarne. We didn't know where you were, but the guards didn't notice you had left. Somehow they must have miscounted. No one but us noticed you were missing, and that wasn't until we got back to the hut and saw your empty bed."

Aarne hadn't considered that. If a prisoner was not accounted for during roll call, all of the other prisoners had to wait in their columns until he was found. Usually guards and dogs went to find the suspected escapee. Usually they found him. The prisoner was dragged back to the square to be tortured or executed in front of the prisoner population, as a warning to the others. He looked at the men around him. They were safe, and so was he.

Today was a new day, and he could start again, struggling to survive along with the other prisoners of Stutthof. He inhaled the spring air. Overhead the pale sun was struggling to take over the sky. He exhaled. He was alive.

CHAPTER 15
Evacuation by Sea, April 1945

—w—

THE BARRACK WAS STILL dark when the guards woke Aarne in the early morning of April 25. Confusion filled his mind as he struggled from his sleep and made his way towards the roll call square. Before dawn nearly the whole camp was organized in tidy columns, just as they had been before January's death march. More than 3,300 prisoners stood at attention, waiting for orders.

This is it, Aarne thought. *They're evacuating us again.* Rumours had it that Himmler himself had ordered that no camps or prisoners could be surrendered to the enemy. Commandant Hoppe and a few others had already abandoned the camp a few weeks before, leaving SS Hauptsturmführer Paul Ehle to organize the evacuation. Aarne knew the Russians were getting closer—so close that their lives were in daily danger from not only the Nazi guards but also the Russian military presence.

Not everyone would be able to begin this journey, Aarne knew. More than a thousand prisoners, ill and dying, were to be left to their fates. Aarne wondered what would happen to them. Would the Nazis kill them? Burn down the camp? Leave them to the Russians?

There was little time to contemplate. Before first light Aarne and his shipmates were on the move again. Some prisoners, he noticed, were loaded into cattle cars, the same type of train he had arrived in many months before. This time, however, his journey to the Baltic was by foot.

—⚏—

After a day and a half of walking, with several inmates succumbing to their illnesses and others brutally beaten or shot en route, they finally reached the mouth of the Vistula River, where they waited for a further two days. More emaciated inmates died. Typhus took several. The SS disposed of those who were too exhausted to move on, including at least a dozen Jewish women who were shot to death in front of the others.

The breeze crossing the river's gleaming surface brought with it the familiar scent of salty sea. Aarne sat on the ground beside Kalevi, letting his arms droop over his knees, his head hung low. His body aching and drained, he could barely make any effort to speak. He closed his eyes, remembering his earlier escape attempt and brief moment of freedom. He remembered the many times the *Wappu* had docked in Danzig, never dreaming he would become a prisoner in a Polish concentration camp.

On so many occasions he had been close to freedom, but each time was followed by new trials to endure. He didn't know if he could go on any longer.

"The war is nearly over," Kalevi said. "That's what everyone is saying."

"Will we ever see the end of this march?" Aarne said.

"It's not the time to give up now. We've come this far."

Aarne nodded. He gazed at the waves lapping against the shore. *But, he wondered, how much farther would they have to go?*

The wait was over. On the night of April 27, Aarne watched a large landing craft pull close to the shore. The guards ordered the prisoners to their feet and forced the inmates to board the boat.

"Get moving," a guard ordered.

The line began to travel quickly. People started running towards the vessel. Aarne heard the guards yelling. Shots rang out. In the distance startled seagulls flapped into the air before settling on some rocks beside the sea to search for their next meal.

Aarne tried to see what was happening, but the backs of prisoners jostling into place blocked his view. He heard a frightened cry followed by a long splash. Someone had fallen or been pushed from the landing craft. As he approached the boat, he heard several more screams as prisoners lost their footing on the slippery surface of the gangway and tumbled into the sea below. He watched as one man struggled to remain afloat, grasping for anything that would help him climb back aboard. He looked up at the guards with frightened eyes and lifted his hand towards one who stared down, emotionless, from the shore. The guard pulled out his revolver. Aimed. Fired. The prisoner slipped soundlessly into the sea.

Shaken, the prisoners waited for the vessel to pull away from shore. Aarne leaned against a wall, his hand touching the smooth surface of the craft, his fingers tracing the outlines of the steel frame. His fingers found a gap in the wall. He reached up to inspect the spot and found a small space. Curious, he stuck his hand inside and felt around. His fingers touched a rough texture that was familiar somehow. He looked around. No one seemed to notice what he was doing. Cautiously he pulled the object from its hiding place in the wall.

Bread. Aarne gasped. Perhaps a soldier had left it behind. It felt a bit hard, but there were no signs of mould.

"Kalevi," Aarne whispered as he blanketed the bread under his jacket. "Look what I found."

Kalevi turned around. His eyes popped open. "You'd better keep that concealed, or someone will take it. Where did you get it?"

Aarne showed him the space. He felt inside again, hoping to find other treasures. It was empty. He knew the bread was more precious than any currency, so he closed his jacket, keeping it close to his chest.

The boat travelled across the Baltic for several kilometres, leaving behind Vistula Bay for Hel Peninsula. Aarne breathed in the sea air. Briefly he closed his eyes, shutting out the ragged bodies lying listlessly on deck, ignoring the stench of sweat and urine. He listened for the sounds of the waves crashing against the sides of the boat and the birds squawking above. When they finally arrived, the SS guards ordered them off the vessel, threatening the prisoners who moved too slowly. One by one they ran back down the gangplank to the sandy shore.

Aarne disembarked and joined a column with the other Finns. Was this still Poland? No one was telling them anything. They began a tedious march across the fine sand, past the dune grass, and into the interior of the isthmus, where they entered a forest, the trees creating long shadows. Eventually a large, open area appeared in the middle. The prisoners gathered in an enclosed space surrounded by a barbed-wire fence.

"It's like we are some kind of cattle, always needing to be fenced in," Aarne heard someone say.

"To them we are. No better than animals, anyway," another replied.

Aarne found a place to stretch his legs on the fresh grass. He wondered how long he and the other inmates would be here. There was no shelter to speak of, and they hadn't eaten anything for days. He would have to make the bread he found last for as long as he could.

The sky above was darkening as the sun began its descent. The forest around the enclosure looked ominous and filled with night sounds. He tried to rest. Sleep seemed impossible. The human sounds of suffering were interspersed with the occasional screeches of birds and the rustle of feet in the underbrush. He heard moans nearby.

As he began to drift to sleep, Aarne imagined himself on another island far away. He and his friends had taken their little boats to one of the islands. He remembered his excitement as they pulled the boats up along the shore, gathered branches and twigs, and knelt to build a fire. The smoke began to rise, and a small flame caught in a quick burst. Aarne fed a few more branches to the growing fire.

The boys sat around, watching the flames crackle and dance. They cooked the small meals they had packed from home, carefully rotating their food so as not to let anything burn. *Nothing ever tasted so good*, he thought as he ate his meal in the fresh air with his friends. The boys told jokes and stories, the fire bursting and snapping as the sun began to set. One by one the stars appeared, sparkling against the night's navy canvas until it was filled with tiny dots, too many to count. He was sleepy, but he couldn't keep his eyes closed, not with the growing sounds of the forest coming alive around them. Everything seemed amplified: the waves, the crackles of the fire, the forest noises. One of the boys began to moan.

"What's wrong?" Aarne asked, lifting himself on his elbow.

The boy looked at Aarne and his friends.

"My tooth! I think I have a toothache," he replied. "I hate to leave this place, but I think I need to go home.

"Home? Of course." The other boys began to pack up their gear and drag it to their boats.

Aarne pulled his boat into the water, thankful for the toothache, which meant his own bed and an escape from the island with all of its unusual sounds.

He startled awake. It had been only a dream, but it seemed as vivid as the night he had rowed home in the dark. Now there was no escaping this night in the forest. He looked around at the figures of his friends asleep on the dirt nearby.

Without warning the distinct droning of airplanes above disrupted the quiet of the evening. Startled, he looked up. They were flying low. Very low. One glance and he knew they were Russian aircraft. Prisoners awoke and scattered, running into the forest to escape the inevitable deployment of bombs. Aarne stumbled on the uneven ground. People screamed. Feet pounded the earth. The prisoners cowered together, some faces raised to scan the sky while others covered their heads, knees and arms balled together under the canopy of the trees. Explosions echoed in the forest and reverberated through the ground. The assault lasted several minutes.

When the air raid stopped, Aarne left his hiding place, looking for his shipmates. Others did the same, calling out names to find their loved ones. He could hear shocked screams as family members and friends recognized the deceased.

Aarne joined the group of Finns, looking around at the familiar faces, so pale and thin. His hands shook from the shock.

"We're OK," a sailor said. He looked around. "I don't think they got any of ours."

The Finnish sailors looked dazed but uninjured. The terror from the bombings dissipated, and the prisoners found places to sit on the bare ground. Aarne scanned the enclosure. Several dead. More injured. The Finns huddled together.

Aarne slept fitfully for a few hours before the guards ordered the columns on their feet again. A slow march from the forested enclosure brought them back to the shore.

He could make out the shapes of three river barges—the *Wolfgang*, the *Vaterland*, and a third barge, all attached to tugboats. The closer he got to the shore, the more dilapidated the vessels looked. They were several feet wide, with small rooms at their fronts for the barge operators. Large doors opened on the flat roofs for stowing goods and materials. In this case, Aarne realized, humans would be the cargo.

"How far do you think we're going to get in these things?" he asked Kalevi. "They look like they're about to sink."

Kalevi agreed. "Maybe that's the idea."

Despite his trepidation, and with no other choice, Aarne stepped into the overflowing *Wolfgang* with the hundreds of other prisoners who were already jammed inside. The interior of the barge was swarming with inmates vying for spaces to sit or lie down. Aarne and Kalevi decided to stay on deck. They picked their way over bodies strewn across it until they found a small spot in the corner, preferring the fresh air and open sky to the crowded interior and its palpable stench.

"Kalevi, take this," Aarne whispered. He handed Kalevi a piece of the bread he had hidden in his jacket.

"Kiitos," Kalevi said. He smiled weakly and accepted the bread.

When the vessels were filled to more than capacity, the tugboats pulled them away from the peninsula. Too tired to talk, the two watched the shoreline disappear in the distance as they sucked on small pieces of the stale bread, trying to be careful not to draw the attention of the starving people around them. They would surely be pounced on if others knew they had food aboard the barge.

The *Wolfgang* sailed westward on its long journey towards Germany. Nearby the two other barges began their voyages. Aarne stared at the sky. He located the Big Dipper and scanned his eyes up to the handle until he found Polaris, the North Star. It was said to be a sailor's friend, its compass leading him to true north, a beacon that held the promise of delivering a ship safely home. It was the only constant in the night sky. But how could it help him this time, as his barge floated somewhere in the Baltic, far away from his northern home?

—⁓—

For the next few days, Aarne and Kalevi stayed together on the deck of the vessel. The interior of the barge was crowded, dirty, and foul. Sweat and vomit mixed with urine and feces. Although it was cold and damp in the outer section, the salty sea air seemed more desirable than the stale, rancid innards of the ship's bowels below. The conditions were inhumane: no food, no water, and no sanitation.

Aarne and Kalevi looked up from their space in the corner of the deck to see the guards carrying a body to the edge. Someone must have succumbed in the night to hunger or disease. The guards stripped the dead man of his clothes, revealing a form more skeletal than human. The body was flung over the side of the boat with ease. The last sound he made was a horrific splash as he hit the water before slipping into the sea and sinking into its depths. For a moment Aarne wondered if the body the guards were tossing over was still breathing; his eyes were wide from malnutrition and fear.

On the third night of the sea voyage, thunder rumbled through the air, and lightning shattered the night sky. A powerful tempest tossed the barge up and down. He heard the retching sounds from prisoners around him, but few had anything left in their stomachs. He closed his eyes as the barge rolled with the motion of the sea. A downpouring of much needed rain was a welcome relief. Aarne had no container to collect the water, so he tried to capture the rainfall with his cupped hands raised to the heavens, slurping as much as he could gather in his palms. Soon his clothes were so waterlogged, he sucked them dry.

For several days a tugboat pulled the *Wolfgang* across the Baltic, arriving in Stralsund on April 30 and Warnemünde on May 1. On May 2 Aarne's barge finally reached its destination: Neustadt, Germany.

—m—

After many gruelling days on the brutal barge, Aarne was relieved to be docked in the harbour. A variety of vessels were already anchored in Lübeck Bay. The *Wolfgang* and other barges moored alongside two large ships. Aarne looked over at the *Thielbeck*, a 273-foot freighter. Close by sat the massive black and red *Cap Arcona*, a large passenger ship that, in her glory days, was called the Queen of the South Atlantic. She had once travelled between Germany and South America. Another passenger ship, the *Deutschland*, had travelled between Hamburg, Southampton, and New York. Close to shore the *Athen*, a smaller freighter, was waiting to transport a group of prisoners to one of the larger ships.

Aarne surveyed the bay, the ships, and the crowds of prisoners. Chaos.

"Looks like we aren't the only ones here," a Finnish sailor said, nodding towards the town of Neustadt.

Crowds of dishevelled and emaciated prisoners lined the shores. Blue and white striped uniforms dotted the landscape. "What do you think they're going to do with all of us?" Aarne whispered. He watched the prisoners boarding the *Athen*.

"My guess is those prisoners are headed for the ships," the sailor said matter-of-factly.

In fact the two large passenger ships anchored in the bay already housed several thousand prisoners from KL Neuengamme and Stutthof's filial camp in Gdynia.

"Maybe they'll bring it out to sea and sink it," the sailor mused. He looked at Aarne's shocked face. "But they're probably just transporting them to another port in Germany."

Aarne did not feel reassured.

—∿—

The SS secured the barges in the harbour. Late that night, Aarne and some of the other prisoners aboard the *Wolfgang* were unable to sleep. They noticed the guards getting on a tugboat and cruising to the small town of Neustadt, a few kilometres in the distance, under the cover of darkness. The prisoners began to whisper and point at the departing guards.

Aarne watched the tugboat chug across the dark bay, the sounds of German voices fading into the distance. Was the barge unattended? Aarne considered their quarters at the front of the vessel. *They must have some kind of kitchen or food storage*, he thought. He glanced again at the tugboat as it shrunk in the distance. Sometimes, he remembered, he had seen the SS men casually throwing empty food tins overboard during the day. There had to be food aboard this barge. One last glance at the tugboat, a small dot at the shoreline, and he turned to the front of the barge and carefully climbed over the sleeping, the sick, and the dying.

What if they left some guards on board? he wondered as he approached the pilot's station. He moved slowly, keeping his eye out for a guard, listening for German voices. Nothing. A few steps more, and he would be at the door. He paused. No sounds from within. Occasionally he could hear movement from the barge and the groans of prisoners. He tried the door. Unlocked. He stepped closer, slowly opening it and peering inside. Blackness. Stepping inside, he looked around, ready to bolt at any moment. Gradually his eyes adjusted to the confines of the dark room.

On a small table Aarne found what he was looking for. His mouth watered. He used two fingers to scoop out the contents of the partially eaten tin of meat. He stuck the food into his mouth, licking his fingers to get every last morsel. He couldn't identify the meat, but it didn't matter. It was tasty. More important, it was food. It was the first bit to pass his lips since he and Kalevi had shared the bread many days before. Aarne's shoulders relaxed.

Without warning, in the midst of enjoying his tin can buffet, the vessel listed to the left. He heard a loud crack and the groan of the boat. It felt as though an explosion had rocked the barge.

It was half past four o'clock, and the prisoners were jolted awake. While Aarne was eating, a few of the Norwegians on the *Wolfgang* had also noticed the SS men's departure; they had dropped the barge's mooring lines and managed to drift the vessel to shore with jury-rigged sails and paddles. The explosive shudder Aarne heard was the *Wolfgang* hitting the sand only metres from the shore. Within seconds Aarne felt the barge list sideways into the shallow bay. Nearby the prisoners of the other barges noticed that the *Wolfgang* was drifting towards the shore and also managed to disengage themselves from the ships they were moored alongside. One by one they floated towards the Pelzerhaken beach.

Aarne heard several screams. As the *Wolfgang* tilted, the prisoners panicked. He heard the rush of feet as the prisoners, dazed from their sleep, realized how close they were to the shore. Aarne saw several men jump from the barge. Others followed. The water was shallow. They ran and swam, using their arms to propel them through the cold water towards the beach.

With his can clutched in his hands, Aarne looked for the best way off the barge. The vessel slanted farther. Prisoners ran in all directions, shouting at one another and crying out as they jumped overboard. In the chaos someone knocked Aarne from behind. The tin can flew from his grasp and fell to the floor. Desperate, he tried to reach it as it rolled back and forth along the deck. Several people stepped on his fingers and fell over him as he crawled on his hands and knees in search of the precious tin. He couldn't find it. Finally, after several attempts, he gave up. He struggled to his feet. He left the can and dropped himself overboard, shocked by the coldness of the shallow water against his legs and torso. He headed with the throngs of prisoners to the nearby beach.

Aarne reached the shore, shivering with cold, and sat in the tall dune grass lining the beach. Out at sea prisoners continued to wade through the water. Several lay on the beach, exhausted from the effort. He scanned the beach for someone he knew, another Finnish sailor or a Norwegian policeman, but could not see a familiar face. He was too exhausted to move.

After a time Aarne joined the thousands of prisoners who besieged the port town of Neustadt, desperately searching for food in the burned out buildings. He wandered aimlessly along the cobblestone streets, weakly hoping to find a house or store with food, but to no avail. In a nearby farmhouse, he heard the sounds of chickens and pigs. Interspersed with these inviting sounds, he heard many prisoners yelling at one another in a dozen different tongues, each one desperate. Aarne saw several other inmates also moving towards the farm, hoping to capture the livestock. He realized he had no chance of finding food there; the animals were too few for the massive number of famished prisoners. With his shoulders low and feet dragging, he turned away from the farm.

After a while, too hungry and fatigued to look any further, he decided to find shelter in the long blades of dune grass growing in the sandbanks. Many others had done the same, sleeping close to the beach, too weary to continue. Was this freedom?

In the bay the barges still listed in the sand, packed with the sick and dying who were unable to jump ship with the others. Gentle waves lapped along the beach. The passenger ships loomed on the horizon, filled with prisoners from the concentration camps. Bodies floated in the bay, tugged gently back and forth with the relentless movement of the sea.

Aarne closed his eyes. Tucking himself under the cover of the sand dunes, he waited.

Chapter 16
Lűbeck Bay, May 1945

———

Aarne lay huddled in the dune grass, the fine sand sticking to his face and covering his fingers. The sea reached far into the horizon before blending into the grey sky. Dark, low clouds threatened rain. It took him several moments, but soon he remembered where he was. Memories of the disorder of the previous day returned in jarring flashes.

He heard the yells of German SS men and the hustling feet of hundreds of prisoners. A group of German marine infantry had arrived and were trying to regain some control over the scattered masses. He was too exhausted to run or fight. With great effort he pulled himself from the sand and stumbled towards the other prisoners, who the guards were organizing into columns. There was nowhere to hide. He followed them, urged on by the heavily armed SS men.

Soon the guards who had abandoned the barges the night before joined the German marine infantry, probably still drunk from their night in Neustadt, and attempted to get the prisoners onto the dilapidated vessels. The boats were in such great disrepair after they had struck the sand of the shallow bay that Aarne couldn't imagine they would be salvaged. It was soon clear even to the guards that the barges were in no condition to be moved. Instead the prisoners watched the SS guards sail back to the barges alone. Several shots rang out across the bay as the guards murdered the remaining prisoners.

Aarne waited with his column, shaken by the horrifying scene around him. Emaciated bodies lay on the beach and floated in the shallow water. It was like nothing he had ever seen, even in the concentration camp. The morning air was cool and rainy, and his body shook uncontrollably in his thin clothes.

All of a sudden, a group of Germans in uniforms appeared along the shore about twenty metres from where he stood. The men, SS marines and young naval cadets from the nearby submarine school, lined themselves along the beach. They turned to face the bay, watching inmates wading in the water towards shore. Someone barked an order in German. In unison the men raised their weapons. Terrified, Aarne looked from the Nazis to the struggling men, women, and children. He froze.

Another clipped order. They opened fire. Machine guns and screams filled the harbour as the soldiers massacred more than two hundred prisoners. Bodies lay riddled, face down in the shallow water and sprawled on the white sand of the beach. Then the SS and cadets moved towards the column. Gunfire turned on the weakest inmates.

When the shooting ended, the water was red and littered with hundreds of floating bodies. Dead prisoners were scattered along the beach. Terrified, Aarne turned his gaze from the barbaric sight, following the remaining Stutthof survivors in their column. Guards led them to the local naval school. Several more gunshots echoed as soldiers indiscriminately executed people en route, amid the tramping footsteps of hundreds of people.

They were in complete confusion. Aarne couldn't understand where they were headed or why. He felt like he was in a daze. The carnage in the harbour had traumatized the witnesses. Everywhere Aarne looked he saw confused and fearful prisoners. Family members clung to one another. Some stood alone, distant, vacant.

When the columns arrived at the naval school at noon, Commandant Hoppe himself announced the transportation of the Stutthof prisoners to Flensburg aboard the *Athen*. Aarne turned around yet again for the march back to the harbour, where the *Athen* was waiting. As the prisoners waited on shore, looking weary and distraught, there seemed to be some delays. The *Athen*, a small freighter that would ferry them to one of the larger ships in the harbour, was already filled to overflowing with prisoners from other concentration camps, and Captain Nobmann refused to take the Stutthof prisoners aboard. The guards, however, continued to force the prisoners towards the ship.

Aarne worked his way towards the *Athen*. When his turn arrived, he grabbed the rungs of the ladder with his shaking hands. But before he could continue, the roar of plane engines filled the air. He paused. He looked into the sky. Within moments the blare of the engines amplified as they whizzed over the prisoners' heads, flying so low he felt like he could touch their metal underbellies. Despite the captain's orders, the guards instructed the prisoners to keep moving. Aarne began climbing rung by rung. Seconds later he heard the explosions of bombs dropping on the harbour. Their first target was the *Deutschland*.

A British RAF squadron of four Typhoons dropped their loads on the defenceless *Deutschland* as it sat anchored in the bay. The Typhoon fighter bombers swung low, dived vertically, shot their rockets at the ships in the harbour and then swung back up quickly, dropping their bombs before flying straight up and away. The planes flew so low, engines shrieking through the air, that Aarne instinctively ducked when they passed overhead, as though the bombs were going to graze the top of his head. The next group of planes followed in quick pursuit with the same precision as the first. The scene was a confusion of planes, bombs, and bodies.

Panic intensified. One after another the Typhoons screamed above, bombed the bay, attacked the ships, and shattered the town. Prisoners and guards dispersed in every direction. As the bombers continued to bombard the ships, Aarne scurried off the *Athen*'s ladder and ran into the street behind hundreds of others.

His legs were weak and his breathing laboured. Smoke rose from the ships, and the wind scattered the scent. The whirr of the bombers was punctuated by a succession of explosions, intensified by the sounds of human cries.

The attacks continued as nine more Typhoons targeted the passenger ship *Cap Arcona* and the *Thielbeck*, a large freighter. Both were already filled with concentration camp prisoners. Aarne turned to see plane after plane pummel the ships with bombs. Smoke rose high into the gloomy sky.

Aarne's heart beat against his chest as he sought shelter. Below the cloud cover, the Typhoons continued their attack. Across the bay he could see flames consuming the *Cap Arcona*, dark smoke joining the grey clouds in the sky. The ship blazed. Prisoners struggled to escape the burning vessel, but many were trapped in the cargo holds.

Four more Typhoons attacked the *Thielbeck*. Unlike the *Cap Arcona*, it didn't burn immediately. Within twenty minutes of the attack, the *Thielbeck* listed and sank into the cold waters of the Baltic.

The onslaught continued for more than an hour. Another eight Typhoons appeared on the horizon, firing more rockets on the already disabled *Deutschland*. Explosions resounded as smoke curled from the ship. Another attack on the *Deutschland* occurred soon after, with two more squadrons directly hitting the flaming vessel. Flames engulfed both the *Cap Arcona* and *Deutschland*.

Aarne was stunned. Earlier that morning the ships had been moored safely in the harbour, waiting for more prisoners to become passengers. Now thousands were dead. Somehow he had escaped the fate of the more than seven thousand prisoners. He learned later that while some of the inmates managed to escape the flames and explosions, pulling themselves over the decks and dropping themselves into the freezing sea, the SS shot others who jumped from the burning ships. Many somehow succeeded in getting to shore only to be shot there by SS men, naval cadets, and even some of the townspeople.

Meanwhile, the prisoners scattered in every direction, trying to find refuge. As he moved towards the town, away from the harbour, Aarne noticed Kalevi running the same way. They made eye contact and, without a word, sprinted in the same direction, trying to find a safe place to hide from the bombs that bombarded the city and harbour. Everywhere Aarne looked, he saw people dashing in all directions, looks of terror splashed on their faces.

Soon he was away from the beach, stumbling over the cobblestone streets of Neustadt, searching between the buildings and narrow alleyways for refuge. He watched for Kalevi, but he was nowhere to be seen. Suddenly he felt very alone.

He ran past a few houses lining the streets, looking for a hiding place. At the base of several buildings, he noticed the wire screens for coal chutes. With little thought he opened the next one he saw, squeezed himself into the narrow opening, and slid down into the coal room below. The room was cold and dark, and coal dust floated into the air as he landed on the floor with a thud. But it was safe from the chaos outside. Exhausted and in shock, Aarne heard the explosions, machine guns, shrieks, and shouts fading into the distance. Then he slept.

—⁂—

It was unusually quiet. He opened his eyes. Darkness. His aching head lay against a piece of jagged coal. Dust rose as he moved and settled, still and cautious. He listened. Once in a while, he heard the sound of a solitary rifle shot in the distance, but he heard no fighting in the street. The roar of the bombers was replaced by the whistle of the wind. An eerie stillness replaced the cries of the dying. For a long time, he waited. He propped himself up against the coal pile, breathing in the coal dust in the semidarkness. *Better to be hidden in the cellar for a while, listening for signs of life*, he thought.

Aarne could make out the distinctive rumble of a tank as it passed along the cobblestones on the street above. He blinked his eyes, adjusting to the low light. He could see the shape of the coal chute hatch and looked up, craving the pale sun filtering through the screen. Thin streams of light were briefly darkened as the tank thundered by, blocking the sunlight. He pulled himself to his feet, dusting himself off with his coal-covered fingers and rubbing his mouth and eyes with the back of his hand. He climbed up a pile of coal and pushed his head out of the opening of the chute. The back of the tank grumbled down the narrow street. He glanced in the other direction but saw nothing save a row of silent houses.

A shot fired nearby. Frightened, Aarne instinctively threw his hands up to surrender. Opening his eyes he could see no one and soon realized it was a large stone thrown from the tank's tracks that reverberated against the brick wall of a building down the street. He sighed with relief and lowered his hands.

Aarne took another deep breath to steady his twitching nerves. With as much strength as he could muster, he dragged his frail body through the narrow opening and then rested on his hands and knees for a moment before pulling himself to standing. He closed his eyes and breathed in the fresh air. He looked up and down the road, but he couldn't see a single soul. Where was everyone? What was happening? Was this a dream? Was he dead? In a daze he wandered down the abandoned street.

A shrill whistle sounded in the street ahead. Aarne paused. An extended arm in an olive uniform pointed with a long finger. The arm was attached to a British soldier whose friendly face had the first pleasant expression he had seen in uniform for a very long time. He looked at the soldier, who nodded encouragingly and pointed again. Aarne stared at him for a second, expressionless, then started in the direction. Soon people emerged from every crevice and corner of the town to join him, dragging themselves and others as though in a slow motion dream.

The survivors moved sluggishly, daring no sudden movements as they picked their way through the streets. Several more British soldiers stationed along the route pointed the way. The prisoners converged on Neustadt stadium, near the German submarine school. As Aarne entered the compound, he could see the large oval already filling with several hundred prisoners. They were scattered across the grass, some with their heads resting in their hands, others embracing one another as they found their friends and families, and many crying inconsolably, knowing they would never see their loved ones again.

In a separate area, away from the former prisoners, Aarne noticed that the British soldiers had enclosed the Nazi guards and marine infantry. He looked away from the sight of them.

It's over, he thought. The British had liberated them. It seemed too unbelievable to be true.

—⟋⟍—

In the stadium Aarne looked for his friends. He found the Finnish sailors sitting together in the open field, enjoying the sun on their faces and breathing in the fresh air. He must have looked shocking with his dust-covered face and clothes, but no one seemed to notice. He saw, for the first time in months, smiles on their chapped lips and sparkles in their sunken eyes. Physically they looked downtrodden, but as their shipmates joined them one by one, hope multiplied.

After some rest and exchanging of stories, Aarne remembered he had seen a milk factory on his way to the stadium.

"I think it was over there," Aarne said, pointing towards the town. "Maybe we should see if we can find anything."

"OK. I'll go with you, Aarne. It's worth the walk if we find something," Kalevi said. The others wished them luck.

"Let us know if you find anything to eat or drink," one of the older sailors said.

Aarne's mouth watered at the prospect of fresh milk. The two walked out of the stadium and down the road leading through a section of tall trees. The town's destruction was clearly evident in every direction they looked. Buildings were devastated, barges in ruins, ships destroyed, bodies strewn everywhere. Aarne tried to focus on the cool air and warm sun on his face, avoiding the horrific sights in the harbour.

They walked for several blocks before they found the factory. Somehow the building was still intact, but the door was bolted shut. After many attempts Aarne picked up a rock and pounded on the window. When it broke they climbed into the building, hoping to discover something edible.

"Look here, I found something" Aarne said to his friend.

The two rushed over to some large bags of sugar. At first they tried to pry the bags open with their fingers, but the material was too thick. Aarne searched until he found a piece of steel left lying on the ground. He pierced the enormous bag, letting the sugar pour out into his palm until it overflowed like a waterfall to the ground. His eyes brightened, and his wide grin spread. He licked his fingers, letting the sweet sugar tingle his tongue. He let it fill his palms until it escaped between his fingers. He couldn't remember ever feeling so happy.

"Maybe we should see if we can find some water. We can mix it into a drink," Aarne suggested. They searched the building until they found a faucet. It was still working.

Aarne's small stomach filled quickly.

"Let's go tell the others," he suggested. They lugged bags of sugar back to the stadium with them, finding them heavier than they expected. When they arrived, their crewmates gathered around in excitement. Word spread rapidly, and many others rushed to the factory.

"We'd better be careful about this," Aarne cautioned the sailors. "When a man is hungry, he is worse than a wolf." He guarded his sugar bag, trying to keep it hidden from view.

As they waited in the stadium, they noticed British soldiers moving amongst the prisoners, giving directions. A friendly looking soldier dressed in a tidy khaki uniform came to talk to the Scandinavians, about 370 of them, and explained they should go to the naval school, where they would be housed in the marine barracks alongside other Finns and Norwegians.

"Don't let anyone else in. These barracks will be just for you. The others will have their own assigned housing," the officer explained. They understood. Many Germans were trying to escape punishment and were pretending to be prisoners. The British didn't want the Germans blending in with the Scandinavians and escaping to Sweden.

The tired men picked themselves up off the ground and made their way to their new accommodations. On the way Aarne noticed some SS men in their ties and fancy uniforms, digging large trenches to bury the victims of the Neustadt massacre. At first the SS dug with their uniforms on, but eventually they threw off their hats, jackets, and shirts as they became stained with sweat and dirt. Soon, he noted with satisfaction, they would be almost as dirty looking as the prisoners.

Inside the naval school barracks, he found a place to sleep under a table. All night he slept with his arms wrapped firmly around his prized sack of sugar.

—⚓—

The next morning Aarne and some of the other prisoners wandered around the marine school, scrounging for food or anything useful. Part of the school contained a large swimming pool with a partial submarine at the bottom for training the cadets. In one of the rooms, he saw a wooden desk, probably belonging to a naval officer. He reached to the handle of the top drawer and opened it. Inside were a German Luger, a Nazi officer's knife, and some ammunition. He looked around. He was alone. He carefully put the gun in his pants, hid the knife, and pocketed the ammunition, not knowing if he would have cause to use them in the future. He told no one.

He continued his search of the rest of the building. It was clean and tidy, a well-organized military facility. In one room, perhaps a classroom, he saw several intricate model ships and submarines of varying sizes. They fascinated him. He studied the different ships, comparing the various models. After a while he selected the smallest one, about thirty centimetres in length, and kept it close to him. It would eventually travel to Sweden and then home to Finland. Someday it would even travel with Aarne to Canada.

After all the prisoners had endured, the British gave them free range in the town of Neustadt. Aarne and his friends scavenged the town and stole whatever they could, looking for food in abandoned houses and buildings. Sometimes they were lucky and found a bit of food stored in a cupboard. Mostly the houses were empty, their residents having fled before the Allies arrived. The horrific moments of May 3 were evident as they passed thousands of corpses scattered on the streets, on the beach, and in the bay.

One day Aarne and his friends found out about a wine cellar in the submarine school that had a large quantity of cigarettes and wine.

"I don't know if this is a good idea," he said. "Most of us are still weak and aren't eating much."

"Don't worry, Aarne. We'll just have a little drink," he was reassured.

Inside the dark cellar, the men found boxes and boxes of wine lining the walls. Someone uncorked the first bottle with a pop. The men cheered. The bottle was passed around from person to person. Everyone was so weak, after a few swigs some of the men passed out.

With all of that wine, the men decided they would use it for something other than drinking.

"We could take baths in it," someone suggested. Several men carried the wine and poured it into the bathtub.

When it was Aarne's turn, he lowered himself into the wine bath. In no time the cold seeped into his skin. He got out quickly, dried himself off, and tried to warm up again.

Since drinking it was of no use, and bathing in it was too cold, a few of the sailors decided to use the wine to wash the floors of the school. All of the mops and everything they needed were available to them, so they sanitized the floors with wine.

After several days of waiting in the submarine school, the sailors began to wish for news from the outside world. The British promised the

Red Cross would soon arrive, but the sailors had little information about the rest of the world. Aarne heard that a few French people had found a radio, so he brought them some wine bottles to make a trade. When he returned to the barracks, the sailors were thrilled. He fiddled with the radio's knob, tuning into mostly German stations until he found one from England. Finally they would make their first contact with the outside world.

For over a week, Aarne and his shipmates lived in the naval school barracks. There was not much to do, but they had food and water, a place to sleep, and a sanitation system. Better yet they were free to come and go, and, after all they had lost during their experiences, they were permitted to take anything they found in the town. And the army supplied soup that was suitable for the strained digestive systems of the prisoners.

As the days progressed, Aarne and some others were beginning to gain strength. They found abandoned cars and bikes and used them to amuse themselves. The British did their best to keep the concentration camp survivors from leaving town as they waited for the Red Cross to arrive. Many wanted to find their own ways home, but it was still too unsafe. Only a few British soldiers were left in Neustadt after the liberation to maintain order with the people. Although the ex-prisoners were able to go anywhere they wanted on their own, they were still expected to stay in their designated barracks at night. The British soldiers also had weapons and were willing to threaten the former prisoners if they tried to pass outside of the town limits. Apart from this restriction, the soldiers left the prisoners to do as they pleased.

One day Aarne and a friend were wandering through town, searching abandoned buildings. They entered what looked like an empty house. Aarne was startled when he found a German lady packing a suitcase. She seemed to be in a great deal of hurry.

"Do you have any food?" he asked, motioning eating with his hands.

The woman shook her head.

"Can you open the cupboards?" Aarne pointed to the cabinets in the kitchen. She opened the doors, exposing the bare shelves.

Aarne scanned the house. It was evident the woman was in the process of packing a suitcase. She was clearly very anxious to leave. On the walls of her home, pictures of her husband and son, dressed smartly in their SS uniforms, smiled out from the frames. *No wonder she wants to leave Neustadt,* he thought. He would have liked to ask where she could possibly be going, but he didn't speak enough German. She hurried out the front door, clutching her lone suitcase, leaving the men to scavenge through her house.

A few days later, two German submarines came into the harbour. The prisoners were fascinated and wanted to take a closer look, but the British soldiers stood at the shore, refusing to let them near the submarines, afraid of what they might do to the German crew. Aarne tried to get a look at it. It was clearly a German submarine, and Lübeck Bay was probably its home port. Once they entered the harbour, the German marines quickly surrendered. *They probably have nowhere else to go,* he thought. Of course the British wouldn't let the ex-prisoners anywhere near them. He lost interest and wandered down the beach to the barracks.

The days were slow, and Aarne longed to go home. He wondered when the Red Cross would arrive to deliver them to Finland. So many people were still sick and dying. Many needed medical care. Their bodies could not adjust to the food, and they ate too much too fast. Once he saw a group make a fire on the platform of the railroad station near the barracks. They used a piece of metal over the fire to fry some fresh eggs from a nearby farm. He was intrigued by their ingenuity, but he was also very cautious. He had seen others around him gorge themselves on food; they weren't used to eating so much. For a long time, Aarne drank his water and sugar combination and ate small portions of food and the soup the military provided. After surviving for so long, he could not consider doing something foolish now that he was finally free.

Waiting for the Red Cross gave him hope that soon he would leave this madness behind. At the time he did not realize that of the 3,300 prisoners who had evacuated Stutthof, 2,000 of whom had sailed by barge from Hel, he was one of only 900 survivors. He was lucky to be alive.

Aarne dreamed of a reunion with his brothers, his sister, and his parents. Every day his hopes for a safe return home grew stronger, but somehow it seemed still a distant dream.

CHAPTER 17
Finland, June 1945

—⁕—

THE RED CROSS FINALLY arrived in big trucks, ready to transport the Scandinavians and other survivors to Denmark. The workers distributed food and other items, provided medical care to the sick, and attended to the dying. When the time came to board the trucks and leave Germany behind, Aarne was nowhere to be seen.

He was rowing a small boat beneath the bridge on the canal leading from the harbour to a small inland lake of sorts. He had often spent time on the water, letting the waves bounce his small boat, feeling the strength return to his arms as he rowed. He loved the smell of the sea in his nostrils and the sun's rays on his face.

"Aarne, it's time to go." He heard a familiar voice calling to him.

He looked up. Kalevi was waving his arms at him, calling him in to shore. He began rowing frantically.

"Don't leave without me! I'll be right there," he shouted across the water.

Aarne jumped from his boat and ran into his barrack to grab his few belongings. By the time he joined the group, his breath was laboured, but he smiled broadly. The former prisoners lined up near the Red Cross vehicles while one of the personnel gave instructions.

"Please leave any nonessentials behind. We won't have much space," he instructed.

Aarne felt his trousers for the gun and ammunition he had hidden. As he approached the truck, he reluctantly surrendered them to the Red Cross. The SS officer's knife with the Nazi insignia, however, he kept hidden from view. He hoped he wouldn't need it.

"Can I keep this model?" He held up the submarine he had stolen from the classroom. The Red Cross worker looked puzzled, but shrugged.

"Yes, I don't see why not," he said.

Aarne had heard that some of the people had looted valuables from the town and instead of giving them up, they placed them into containers and buried them in the ground, believing they might return to retrieve their treasures someday in the future. How they would ever be able to find them again was beyond comprehension.

Once he was on the truck, Aarne sat with Kalevi and his shipmates. Already many of them were looking healthier and certainly happier. Aarne was eager to go to Denmark; it was that much closer to his own country. A volunteer arrived, passing machine guns to some of the survivors.

"What are these for?" Kalevi asked, his eyes questioning.

"We don't anticipate any problems, but the area is still volatile. It's better to be protected, don't you think?"

The truck rumbled against the cobblestone streets, jostling its passengers.

"Yes, of course," he said, taking the machine gun and placing it near his seat. Aarne wondered if he should have kept the German Luger after all.

He looked back to see the barracks fading in the distance. As the truck made its way down the sloping road, past the train station, he took one last look at the harbour where it opened up into the Baltic sea. An image of the Typhoons flying overhead, the ships blazing in the bay, and the smoke spiralling into the sky flashed before him. He imagined he could smell smoke and coal dust rising in the air. Shifting positions, he turned his back on Lübeck Bay.

Travel was long and tedious but did not compare to the poor conditions on the train to Stutthof or the death march away from it. The Red Cross trucks regularly stopped for the former prisoners to stretch their legs, use the facilities, and eat. For the first time in months, he felt that he was being treated like a human being.

Over time the landscape changed. The devastation from the war was evident in the forests, fields, and towns. Buildings were in ruins; the roads were full of potholes from explosions. Everywhere displaced persons struggled with their few belongings. *It could be a long time before life gets back to normal, if ever,* Aarne thought.

—⚍—

When they finally arrived at the Danish border, Kalevi pointed to a group of German soldiers.

"Look there," he said. "It looks like they're being forced to surrender everything."

Aarne nodded. He observed the faces of the German soldiers. Some looked distraught. Others were smiling. Perhaps they were just as relieved as the prisoners were that the war was over. Trucks were piled high with machinery and military equipment. So much had changed.

A spirit of happiness permeated the truck as they entered the country. When they arrived in Helsingør, the Scandinavian sailors were delighted by the Danes who greeted them, offering them flowers. Aarne buried his face in a delicate bouquet. The sweet scent was unlike anything he had smelled for many months, even years.

From Denmark the Finns went to Norrköping, Sweden, where they stayed in a makeshift hospital and had their health assessed. They soon stripped off the filthy clothes they had worn for the past many months. Hospital personnel burned the old garments.

Aarne showered, enjoying the clean water and soap, and put on fresh hospital clothes. A doctor conducted a medical examination and placed him on a treatment plan until he was strong enough to go home.

Most of the Finns were put on a special liquid diet that provided them with lots of nutrition until they could handle other types of food. Aarne was grateful for the doctors and nurses who cared for them, but despite the excellent attention to their health, three of the Finnish sailors died in the hospital. Some suffered from raging fevers. Others' enervated bodies rejected the carefully designed treatments.

Aarne was devastated. He lay in his hospital bed, wondering how this could have happened. After surviving the concentration camp, the death march, and the naval evacuation, he couldn't understand how his shipmates could live to see liberation only to succumb in the hospital.

—⁓—

Sweden's night sky dazzled Aarne. For many years, since the war had begun, most of Europe was enveloped in darkness. Now, with the war over, the lights shone brightly, the sea reflecting the glimmer of the city in an array of colours like he couldn't remember ever seeing. It was an amazing sight to behold. Sweden was glowing.

When he recovered, Aarne and some of his fellow Finnish sailors left the Swedish hospital. But before they went home, the sailors selected new clothes from a local store. All of the choices overwhelmed Aarne.

"What do you think?" he asked his friends as he strutted out in a dark suit and tie, a fresh white shirt, and shiny shoes. He briefly remembered the Sunday shoes he wore from the ship and the stolen jackboots. When he put on his new shoes, he felt like a new man. With his health returning and a fresh set of clothes, Aarne was enthusiastic to be going home finally.

From the Swedish hospital, they travelled over the Baltic to Turku, Finland. As they arrived several journalists, knowing the sailors from Stutthof were aboard the ship, greeted them in the harbour, anxious to question the men about their experiences. By that time stories of the atrocities of the concentration camps had reached countries around the world. The sailors disembarked, smiling at the small crowd that gathered to meet them, relieved to be stepping back onto Finnish soil.

One of the first people they met on their arrival as they left the gangplank of the ship was a Finnish reporter.

"Tell me what happened to you, the crew of the S/S *Wappu*," the reporter said, sharply dressed in a crisp blouse, dark skirt, and blazer. Her short curls swept her furrowed brow as the Baltic breeze gathered strength. Her pen hovered over her notepad.

One of the senior sailors told her their harrowing tale, ending with the tragic details of losing some of their crewmates while in the Swedish hospital.

"I don't believe you," the reporter said. "This is impossible. This didn't happen." She looked accusingly at the men. Her smile faded, replaced by pursed lips, lines gathering in the corners of her mouth as though drawn like cat whiskers.

"You don't believe us?" the sailor responded. "How dare you."

How was it possible that this reporter would question their honesty, after all they had been through these many months? Aarne watched as his shipmate's anger rose. The man clenched his fists, his knuckles whitening as the colour on his face darkened. He and his fellow sailors had looked starvation and death in the eyes; they had lost friends and almost died themselves. They had survived the most appalling conditions and lived to tell about it. In his rage the sailor stepped towards the reporter, grabbed her notebook, and threw it into the harbour.

Shocked, the reporter turned on her heels, which clacked against the cobblestones away from the gathering crowd of reporters and citizens.

The reporter's reaction was Aarne's first indication that not everyone was going to welcome them home with open arms.

From Turku, the sailors believed, they would be going home. The Red Cross had provided them with clothes and enough money to travel, but the authorities had another idea. Aarne and the others took a train from Turku to Hanko where the police promptly detained them. The men were angry.

A barbed-wire fence cordoned off a section of the police yard, and several people were already in its confines.

"We're not going in there," a sailor said. He motioned to the enclosure where the police were directing them.

"You will be in quarantine before being released," an officer explained.

"No. We have just come from the hospital, and we've been cleared. There's no way we're going in there and catching some disease now that we're healthy. We're going home."

The other sailors nodded in agreement. The Finnish sailors would have nothing to do with these new arrangements.

"You will be questioned about your whereabouts during the war," the officer said. "It is strict protocol for all returning Finnish citizens."

The sailors were provided a separate area to wait before the police interrogated them. Before his turn Aarne joined the others to discuss their situation, shocked to be put in this position and angry that the police were holding them under the auspices of a quarantine. Their conversation turned from irritation to outrage.

"We've already spent weeks in the Swedish hospital. We've been treated and cleared of any illnesses. The doctors in Sweden wouldn't have released us if we still carried diseases. There's no reason why we should be quarantined again," a sailor said.

"They're not quarantining us. They think we've done something wrong. Maybe they think we are one of *them*."

"Who knows what they think?" another said.

"Don't tell them anything," an older sailor advised. "Just tell them your name and where you are from. They have no reason to keep us here. We are not cooperating with these people."

Aarne agreed. When it was his turn, he followed the officer into the stark room, a wooden table and chairs its only furniture. A naked bulb hung from the ceiling, casting a stark glow over the proceedings, like in a scene from a movie. He was tired and anxious to go home to Oulu. He was desperate to be reunited with his parents and his older siblings. It had been eight months since his imprisonment, but he had not seen his family in years, since he had started working on the S/S *Wappu*. He answered the basic questions: his name and address, his father's name and occupation, his level of schooling, and where he had been detained. He offered no further information about life in Stutthof.

"I am Aarne Kovala from Oulu, Finland," he said. His determined voice told the policeman he had nothing else to say. He looked directly at the accusing officer, his pale-blue eyes unblinking.

"You are a Communist." The officer slapped both palms against the table. He pressed his hands against its surface as he leaned over Aarne, glaring into his eyes.

Aarne repeated his statement, trying to contain the anger surging from his belly. He just wanted to go home.

"We think you were working with the Nazis. Maybe you *are* a Nazi. Tell us everything." The stern man spoke in a rapid succession of Finnish words, much like the harsh, rapid-fire voices of the Germans who had imprisoned him for those many months.

Aarne stared at the shiny buttons of the Hanko police officer's attire, remembering the dirty clothes he had worn for months on end, the putrid smell that seeped through the thin threads, the lice that congregated and would not disband. He had finally discarded and destroyed his clothes after he had arrived at the hospital in Sweden. The officer's uniform was pressed and tidy; it smelled fresh and clean. His boots shone with polish.

Aarne sighed, the anger seeping away, resigned to more questioning as the time passed endlessly. He sat back in his chair, rolling a piece of paper between his thumb and forefinger. Nothing he said would make a difference to this man who knew nothing of his experiences. He would not believe Aarne, not even if Aarne told him every detail of the horrific truth. He did not want to hear the truth. The truth was too atrocious, too unbelievable.

Aarne knew the Hanko police were also questioning his friends. These men, fellow shipmates from the *Wappu*, were finally in their own country, only their own countrymen were preventing them from going home.

As the night wore on and the pale light of dawn crept through the windows, drawing thick yellow lines on the wooden planks of the station floor, the police finally relented.

"You have no reason to keep us here," Captain Vihtori Jansen said. "We have done nothing wrong."

The other sailors agreed.

"You are free to go," the officer replied. Resigned, the police, having questioned each man in turn, knew they could no longer hold the crew of the *Wappu*. They had nothing with which to indict them; all of their accusations were unfounded. Individual interviews confirmed the details of the sailors' imprisonment in Stutthof. Satisfied, the Hanko police finally released their detainees.

The men gathered their few belongings and filed through the door, to the street in front of the police station, the sun slowly peeking through the birch trees, beginning to warm the early June morning. The men shook hands before departing, their warm clasps lasting longer than the usual handshakes. They exchanged few words. Each man turned in his own direction, all headed towards families and loved ones who were spread across the small northern country.

For the first time in nine months, freedom was truly theirs. But it would not come without a price. Months of hiding food and waking from nightmares, feelings of distrust and guilt at having survived while others had not, would invade their daily lives. There was no one who could understand what had happened to them save those who had lived through it. Judging by the reactions of those they had already met, people might have a hard time believing them, even if they were able to share the horrors they had endured. And they were the lucky few, the survivors. For now home meant peace at long last.

Aarne paused to watch the sun rising in the east, its long fingers spreading through the new green leaves of the white birch trees. The waves lapped gently on the shore, dancing and glistening in the sunlight. As he had done before, he went alone to the train station.

It was June 10, 1945, Aarne's seventeenth birthday.

He was finally going home.

Afterword

THE STORY YOU HAVE just read belongs to my father, Aarne Kovala. Every Sunday through the winter months and the thaw of the spring, my father and I travelled together through decades and countries, down rivers and across oceans. When his stories came to a close, I felt a deep desire to journey to the places of his past. In the summer of 2013, I travelled to Gdańsk, Poland, previously Danzig, and Lübeck, Germany, to touch the soil where my father once walked.

My travels brought me first to the reconstructed port of Gdańsk, where my father's ship was detained and the sailors arrested. From there I took a comfortable motor coach from the train station, past the urban sprawl, through flat fields, and over wide rivers. The bus twisted into a dark pine and fir forest. I couldn't help but feel chills when I noticed the narrow railway tracks outside my window, paralleling the road for many kilometres. Was this the track that had brought my father to Stutthof?

From the bus stop, I backtracked to the small railway station. Across the quiet, tree-lined road, tall grass waved in a rolling field. A cobblestone street led me along a brick and wood fence until I finally arrived at Stutthof.

So much has been destroyed since my father was incarcerated there, but what remains tells the horrific story of the daily lives of prisoners and the guards' cruel treatment. My guide, Stanislaw, himself a Polish concentration camp survivor, expertly guided me through the death gate and into the barracks. Everything he shared about the camp reminded me of my father's stories. I paused in the place where his barrack once stood overlooking the crematory, a view of the dense forest in the distance. I imagined what it must have been like for him and his countrymen, and knew I could never truly understand what they had gone through. I could only imagine. As my tour came to a close, Stanislaw embraced me with tears in his eyes. As if on cue, dark clouds rolled in, and the heavens opened.

—⁂—

Insight into my father's experiences came when we travelled together to Washington, DC, in the summer of 2012, to fulfil his decades-long desire to visit the United States Holocaust Memorial Museum, a place honouring the victims of the Hitler regime. For months he poured out his stories like coffee from a thermos, eager finally to share them with a willing listener. Now he would fill himself up again with the stories of the millions of others who experienced the unimaginable, finding some solace in the shared experience, the acknowledgement of his pain, the understanding that none are forgotten.

Near the end of our visit, we stood together in the glass corridor overlooking the Hall of Witness. I traced my finger over the smooth glass, outlining the white letters etched on the window. As we walked down the corridor, my father and I scanned the endless rows of names that reached from above my head to the soles of my shoes, every word the first name of a person that perished during the Holocaust. I paused midway across the bridge and took a deep breath. The window was cool to the touch, but a midafternoon light streamed through the glass wall of the vaulted ceiling to warm my face. I blinked back tears as I searched the cloudless sky above for answers. There were none.

For several metres on both sides, and behind on the opposite wall of the glass corridor, the names stood between us and the scene on the other side. Through the window below the suspended corridor, streams of nameless visitors—parents with their children, groups of teens, seniors carrying canes and pushing walkers—of every colour and ethnicity entered the main floor, faces lit by the sunshine flooding the room, surrounded by the red brick walls and dark-grey steel beams that form the walls of the museum. The Hall of Witness looked like a prison, imposing and oppressive, yet the light illuminated the walls and floor, bouncing off the steel rails of the staircase. On the opposite wall I read, "You are my witnesses" in white block letters against a dark slate wall.

I caught a glimpse of our reflections in the glass, but we were not the same people who had started this journey together so many months before. From the hall below, a solitary face turned up towards me. I stood beside my father on the bridge, above this stranger. For a brief moment, our eyes locked. She did not yet know that she too would become a witness; before the day was done, her reflection would also have changed, and the white names etched on the glass would be imprinted on her soul forever, as they are on mine.

—ᴡᴡ—

203

In our final meetings, my father filled in details about his life, returning at times to stories he had already shared, clarifying and expanding. While I was fortunate to hear firsthand the story of my father's early life, I know there is so much more that has long since been lost in his memory or is too painful to recount. Only now that I have recorded the details and travelled to Poland and Germany do I connect all of the pieces together into a whole. It is the end of a long voyage of discovery and the beginning of a new understanding. Every cup of coffee we shared, every photo we perused, every document we pored over, gave me a glimpse into his past and made a stronger connection in the present, a gift that easily could have slipped away without a willing storyteller and an eager listener.

As my father's stories came to a close, I wondered how liberated he really felt after all he had experienced. After the war my father didn't speak much about his experiences at Stutthof, and few people dared ask. After encountering the news reporter who doubted the sailors' stories and being detained by the authorities in Hanko, he didn't think people would believe what had happened to him and his shipmates. Talking about it brought back painful memories. He told his parents a few details, but he didn't want to cause them anymore hurt than they had already experienced during the war. One of their sons had lost his leg; a second had lost his life. A third had been a prisoner. They had suffered enough.

According to his mother, Anna Liisa, after every meal Aarne saved a plate of food, just in case. His parents never questioned him about it, only wondered how long it would last. Eventually he did stop hoarding food, but his nightmares never stopped. Insomnia settled into its permanent home.

It is clear to me that after almost seven decades, some part of him is still confined beyond the gates, in that camp, where the most unspeakable things happened. Perhaps by telling his story, he is able to inch open the gate, little by little, until he can once again feel the fresh, salty breeze on his face and the waves gently swaying below his feet.

—⁂—

The end of my journey brought me to the beginning of his: a port town in Poland, a train in the forest, a sandy beach on the Baltic. I strolled along the cobblestones that were once strewn with debris from bombings in Gdańsk. I walked on the soil where my father's barrack once stood and closed my eyes, imagining him there, in this prison surrounded by barbed-wire fences, encircled by pine forests, his beloved Baltic Sea so far in the distance. In the end a long train trip delivered me to Germany and the place of my father's liberation. I felt the fine, white sand between my toes as I watched laughing children play on the beach in Neustadt, oblivious to the tragic events that had happened there so many decades before. The sparkling, azure water lapped at my feet as the sun beamed in the cloudless sky. A warm breeze rustled the dune grass on the shore. Out at sea a few birds swooped and squawked.

The sounds of freedom.

Author's Note

My FATHER SHARED THE events described in *The Day Soon Dawns* with me over a period of about six months in the winter and spring of 2012. His remarkable ability to recall his carefree childhood and troubling youth astonished me. However, after almost seven decades, some details are lost forever to that indescribable ebb and flow of sea we call memory. As a result, during the writing of this book, I tried my best to fill in the gaps. Some names were changed or fictionalized, conversations were invented and scenes were reimagined. I relied on both research and imagination to recreate a time and place I had not personally experienced. I hoped to recount the spirit of my father's reminiscences with as much accuracy as I could, realizing that memory's deep waters are difficult to hold in one's hands; so often when it is grasped, it trickles through the fingertips and flows away. Wherever I could, I used research to support my father's recollections, relying, for instance, on Janina Grabowska-Chałka's *Guide Historical Information: Museum Stutthof* for factual details about the KL Stutthof. My journey to Poland and Germany was also an invaluable and incredibly moving experience. I am also indebted to the memoirs of other survivors for their detailed accounts of life in the concentration camps and for having the courage to tell their stories. In the end I hope that I have told my father's story in a way that does justice to his memories and honours his experiences.

Notes

Chapter One

2   "The Russians wanted": Trotter, William R. *A Frozen Hell: The Russo-Finnish Winter War of 1939-1940*. Chapel Hill: Algonquin Books, 1991. 283. Print.

Chapter Two

11   "The last air raid": "The Finnish Defence Forces—talvisota." *The Finnish Defence Forces*. The Finnish Defence Forces, 04 12 2012. Web. 06/08/2013. http://www.puolustusvoimat.fi/wcm/ Erikoissivustot/talvisodansahkeet/English/News/Talvisodan.

15   "Finland's small army": *A Frozen Hell: The Russo-Finnish Winter War of 1939-1940*.

20   "Oulu was now a garrison town": "1939-1959—City of Oulu." *Oulu, Finland*. N.p. Web. 23 November 2013. http://www.ouka. fi/oulu/english/1939-1959;jsessionid=D551CBB6B9C4A64E5C E2D76F7CAE9A1F.

Chapter Five

49   "Finland's war with Russia": *A Frozen Hell: The Russo-Finnish Winter War of 1939-1940*.

Chapter Seven

69   "Each barrack was approximately": *Guide Historical Information Museum Stutthof*.

Photo Captions

Acknowledgments

I EXTEND A HEARTFELT thanks to my family, friends, colleagues, and students, too many to list here, who expressed interest and encouraged me during the writing of this book. I am very grateful to my fellow students and my teachers at the University of Toronto's School of Continuing Studies Creative Writing program for their feedback and for sharing their gifts with new writers. In particular, I wish to thank Marina Nemat for inspiring and encouraging me throughout this process. I couldn't have completed this manuscript without the patience of my mentor teacher, Allyson Latta, whose keen eye for details and gentle, guiding spirit made everything better.

My early readers, Francine Jensen, Heini Heinonen-Kari, Roy Kari, and Marybeth Levan gave me invaluable suggestions at various stages of the manuscript. Andrea Levan gave generously of her time to provide thoughtful suggestions and careful editing. Thank you to Carita Lanner for translating my father's letter from its original Swedish. Malla Partala shared family stories, photos, and research and painstakingly translated Finnish documents. Kiitos! Many thanks to Jani Ahlstedt, whose interest in my father's story led to our involvement in his documentary about Finnish internees. Thanks also to Tore Jorgensen, who kindly shared information and entries from his work with the Norwegian policemen's diaries.

Love and thanks to my mom, who initiated this project and gave me the early gift of reading. Most of all, thank you to my father for trusting me to tell his story. It has been an amazing journey. Kiitos!

Last, love to Michael, my first reader, for his unwavering confidence, and to my children, Mia and Kieran, for whom this story was necessary to write.

In addition to reading a wide range of survivor memoirs, the following list of museums, books, websites, and films proved invaluable to my research and understanding of the time period.

Archives of Muzeum Stutthof (Stutthof Museum) in Sztutowo, Poland (AMS).

Aroneanu, Eugène. *Inside the Concentration Camps: Eyewitness Accounts of Life in Hitler's Death Camps.* Westport: Praeger Publishers, 1996. Print.

City Archives and Cap Arcona Museum in Neustadt in Holstein, Germany.

Chan, Oscar, dir. *Nazi Titanic.* A&E Television Networks, 2012. Film.

Drywa, Danuta. *The Extermination of Jews in Stutthof Concentration Camp: 1939–1945.* Gdańsk, Stutthof Museum in Sztutowo, 2004. 378. Print.

Engle, Eloise, and Lauri Paananen. *The Winter War: The Soviet Attack on Finland, 1939–1940.* Stackpole Books, 1992. 192. Print.

"The Finnish Defence Forces—talvisota." *The Finnish Defence Forces.* The Finnish Defence Forces, 04 December 2012. Web. 06 August 2013. http://www.puolustusvoimat.fi/wcm/Erikoissivustot/talvisodansahkeet/English/News/Talvisodan.

Gebacki, Jerzy, dir. *Stutthof,* 1994. Film.

Grabowska-Chałka, Janina. *Guide Historical Information Museum Stutthof.* Stutthof, Gdánsk-Sztutowo: MW, 2011. 158. Print. www.stutthof.org.

"Holocaust Encyclopedia." *United States Holocaust Memorial Museum.* United States Holocaust Memorial Museum, 10 June 2013. Web. 23 November 2013. http://www.ushmm.org/wlc/en/article.php?ModuleId=10005197.

Jacobs, Benjamin, and Eugene Pool. *The 100-Year Secret: Britain's Hidden World War II Massacre.* Guilford, Connecticut: The Lyons Press, 2004. 214. Print.

Jorgensen, Tore. (translator). Excerpts from the Norwegian Policemen's Diaries.

Kogon, Eugen. *The Theory and Practice of Hell: The German Concentration Camps and the System behind Them.* New York: Farrar, Straus and Giroux, 2006. 368. Print.

Maritime Museum of Finland in Kotka, Finland. www.nba.fi/en/museums/ maritime_museum

Megargee, Geoffrey P. (ed.). *Encyclopedia of Camps and Ghettos, 1933–1945.* Volume 1. Bloomington & Indianapolis: Indiana University Press, 2009. 1796. Print.

Muzeum Stutthof w Sztutowie. MuzeumStutthof w Sztutowie, n.d. Web. 23 November 2013. http://stutthof.org/english/node/8.

Nylund, Sven. "Suomalaisten merimiesten internoinnit toisen maailmansodanaikana." Trans. Array *Prisoners of War and Internees: A Book of Articles by the National Archives.* Helsinki: 2008. 430–513. Web. 20 May 2013. http://www.yumpu.com/fi/document/view/5678599/ sotavangit-ja-internoidut/503.

Owsinki, Marcin, Waldemar Szymanski, and Piotr Tarnowski. *Guidebook to Stutthof Museum in Sztutowo.* Sztutowo: Muzeum Stutthof. 15. Print.

Parikka, Pekka, dir. *The Winter War (Talvisota).* Writ. Antti Tuuri, 1989. DVD.

Reponen, Oskar. *Kaasukammion varjossa.* Espoo: Amer-yhtymä Oy Weilin + Göös kirjapaino, 1980. 309. Print.

Przbyblyska, Betty (trans.). *Stutthof Historic Guide.* Gdańsk: Krajowa Agencja Wydawnicza, 1980. Print.

Sruoga, Balys. *Forest of the Gods.* Translated by Aušrinė Byla. Versus aureus, 2013. 410. eBook.

Trotter, William R. *A Frozen Hell: The Russo-Finnish Winter War of 1939–1940.* Chapel Hill: Algonquin Books, 1991. 283. Print.

United States Holocaust Memorial Museum in Washington, DC.

Yla, Stasys. *A Priest in Stutthof: Human Experiences in the World of Subhuman.* New York: Manyland Books, 1971. 294. Print.

1939–1959—City of Oulu. *Oulu, Finland.* N.p. Web. 23 November 2013. http://www.ouka.fi/oulu/english/1939-1959;jsessionid=D551CBB6 B9C4A64E5CE2D76F7CAE9A1F.

Made in the USA
Charleston, SC
20 May 2015